A Dynamic Partnership:

Canada's Changing Role In The Americas

North·South Center
UNIVERSITY OF MIAMI

A Dynamic Partnership:

Canada's Changing Role in the Hemisphere

Edited by
Jerry Haar and Edgar J. Dosman

Transaction Publishers
New Brunswick (U.S.A.) and London (U.K.)

Library of Congress Cataloging-in-Publication Data

A Dynamic Partnership: Canada's Changing Role in the Americas /
Edited by Jerry Haar, Edgar J. Dosman.
    p   cm.
Includes bibliographical references.
ISBN 1-56000-725-7 (paper)
    1. Canada — Foreign relations — 1945- 2. Canada — Foreign relations
- Latin America. 3. Latin America — Foreign relations — Canada.
4. Canada — Foreign relations — Caribbean Area. 5. Caribbean Area -
- Foreign relations — Canada.   I. Haar, Jerry.   II. Dosman, Edgar J.
    F1034.2.D96 1993
    327.71—dc20   93-31330
                                                      CIP

ISBN-1-56000-725-7 (paper)
Printed in the United States of America

CONTENTS

PREFACE

The genesis of this book occurred in early 1992 when the North-South Center of the University of Miami decided to launch the Canada Project. As the only research, public policy studies, and information center of its type exclusively dedicated to finding practical solutions to problems facing the nations of the Western Hemisphere, the Center recognized Canada's unique and important role in the hemisphere vis-à-vis the North-South Center's priority areas: trade, environment, democratization, debt and investment, narcotics trafficking, and social equity.

In formulating an agenda for the North-South Center's Canada Project, one with a multi-year time horizon, the Center decided from the beginning to shun a "Made in the U.S.A." approach and chose, instead, to invite twelve distinguished scholars, ten from Canada and two from the United States, to set the agenda at a two-day conference jointly sponsored by the Center and the Canada-Latin America Forum (FOCAL) in Miami in March 1992. FOCAL seemed the most logical Canadian partner for the North-South Center in this endeavor since the Ottawa-based organization's mission is to lower the cultural distance and other barriers between Canada and Latin America and to foster programs and activities of mutual benefit. FOCAL, like the North-South Center, works with business, government, academic, and non-governmental organizations (NGOs) in areas such as social and political development, commercial relations, democracy and human rights, conflict resolution, the environment, and aboriginal issues. This spirit of partnership which launched the Canada Project (which has since grown significantly and become a full-fledged Program of the North-South Center) has been and will continue to be the guiding principle of interaction between our respective organizations in all present and future ventures.

The chapters in this volume are based on papers presented at the two-day workshop and cover a wide range of timely, relevant, and thought-provoking issues that concern Canada's changing role in the hemisphere. The North-South Center and FOCAL have subsequently been engaged with other Canadian partners, such as the Centre for International Studies at the University of Toronto and the École des Hautes Études Commerciales (HEC) in Quebec, in planning and implementing a full array of significant, new activities, both academic and policy-oriented.

The timing of this volume is propitious, to say the least. Since 1990, Canada has been dramatically changing its orientation and

i

priorities vis-à-vis the Western Hemisphere through its active involvement in the Organization of American States (OAS), in peacekeeping activities, through its role in helping to resolve the Haitian situation, and through increased commercial relations with Mexico as part of the imminent North American Free Trade Agreement (NAFTA). Canada has finally become a truly inter-American participant.

On the domestic front as well, Canada is confronting the changing architecture of North America, politically, socially, economically, and commercially. Governance issues affecting Canada, questions regarding native peoples, immigration, health care and social welfare, employment and the economy are part and parcel of Canada's dilemma in striving to achieve economic growth and improve social equity at home, while playing a responsive and productive role as a medium power with a global vision abroad, particularly in the Western Hemisphere.

The threats, opportunities, challenges, and recognized successes which shape Canada's role in the hemisphere will clearly affect, and be affected by, events in the United States, Latin America, and Canada itself. The essence of Canadian culture and that nation's evolving foreign policy agenda are making an imprint on inter-American relations. This volume is an effort to present, analyze, and anticipate the factors and forces which will continue to affect Canada's evolving hemispheric role.

The editors wish to extend their deep gratitude to Wendy Drukier, Laura Kozloski, and Analorena Tamargo who spent laborious hours assisting with the editing of the volume; Valerie Collins, Nancy Colón, and Norma Laird who also made a significant contribution to the manuscript's preparation; and to Professor David H. Pollock of Carleton University who provided editorial assistance. Finally, we wish to thank the staff and leadership of both the North-South Center and FOCAL for supporting this endeavor and enabling us to come together to organize the workshop and publish this volume in the spirit of close collaboration and mutual respect which we hope will shape not only U.S.-Canadian but also hemispheric relations in years to come.

Jerry Haar   Edgar J. Dosman
Director, Canada Program   Director
North-South Center   Canada-Latin America Forum
                                                          (FOCAL)

ACRONYMS AND ABBREVIATIONS

Andean Pact - Bolivia, Colombia, Ecuador, Peru, and Venezuela

Anglophone - English-speaking

ASEAN - Association of Southeast Asian Nations

Caricom - Caribbean Common Market

CBI - Caribbean Basin Initiative

CCF - Cooperative Commonwealth Federation

CCIC - Canadian Council on International Cooperation

CHF - Canadian Hunger Foundation

CIA - (U.S.) Central Intelligence Agency

CICAD - Inter-American Drug Abuse Control Commission

CIDA - Canadian International Development Agency

CNGSB - Coordinadora Nacional Guerrillera Simón Bolívar

Commonwealth Caribbean - English-speaking countries, including Anguilla, Antigua and Barbuda, Bahamas, Bermuda, Barbados, Belize, British Virgin Islands, Cayman Islands, Grenada, Guyana, Jamaica, Montserrat, Saint Kitts and Nevis, Saint Lucia, Saint Vincent and the Grenadines, Trinidad and Tobago, Turks and Caicos Islands

CUSFTA - Canada-U.S. Free Trade Agreement

CUSO - originally, Canadian University Service Overseas; no longer affiliated with universities

DAS - (Colombia) Departamento Administrativo de Seguridad

DEA - (Canada) Department of External Affairs; (U.S.) Drug Enforcement Agency

EAI - Enterprise for the Americas Initiative

EC - European Community

ECLAC - UN Economic Commission for Latin America and the Caribbean

EDC - Export Development Corporation

FDI - foreign direct investment

FMC - First Ministers' Conference

FOCAL - Canada-Latin America Forum

Francophone - French-speaking

FTA - free trade agreement

GATT - General Agreement on Tariffs and Trade

GDP - gross domestic product

GNP - gross national product

HEC - Ècole des Hautes Ètudes Commerciales (Québec)

IDB - Inter-American Development Bank

IDRC - International Development Research Council

IMF - International Monetary Fund

LAC - Latin America and the Caribbean

MAP - mutual assistance pact

Mercosur - Southern Common Market

MIF - multilateral investment fund

MNC - multi-national company

MRTA - Movimiento Revolucionario Tupac Amaru

NAFTA - North American Free Trade Agreement

NATO - North Atlantic Treaty Organization

NGO - non-governmental organization

NIC - newly industrializing country

NORAD - North American Aerospace Defense Command

OAS - Organization of American States

ODA - overseas development assistance

OECD - Organization for Economic Cooperation and Development

ONUCA - UN Observers for Central America

ONUVEN - UN Observers for Election Verification in Nicaragua

PAU - Pan-American Union

PCIAC - Petro-Canada International Assistance Corporation

PPP - Public Participation Program

RCMP - Royal Canadian Mounted Police

Sendero Luminoso - Shining Path

TRIM - trade-related investment measure

UNCTAD - UN Commission on Trade and Development

WH - Western Hemisphere

WHFTA - Western Hemisphere Free Trade Association

Overview and Introductory Comments

Ann Weston, North-South Institute

The purpose of the papers in this volume is to discuss Canada's "home in the Americas" and identify an agenda for future research. Two hypotheses are explored: 1) Canada and Latin America have a wide range of mutual interests which justify a closer relationship, and 2) Canada has a "new disposition and unique capabilities" (Landau 1990, 23). At issue are what form the relationship will take, how it might be reinforced, and where the United States will fit into this new configuration.

A New Era — A New Model?

The papers were written against a background of momentous changes around the world as well as in the United States, Canada, and the rest of the hemisphere. Whether in terms of economic, social, political, or strategic developments, the Western Hemisphere appears to be on the brink of a new era. Many countries in Latin America have rejected their inward-looking economic development strategies in favor of a more liberal market and outward-oriented path, closer to that followed in the United States and Canada.

The transition is unlikely to be smooth or straightforward. For instance, despite the cut in the Latin American debt/gross national product (GNP) ratio in 1991 to just above the 1980 level and the halving of the debt-servicing ratio to 23 percent in 1991 (nearly half the peak of 41 percent reached in 1982), questions remain about the adequacy of resources for development and about persisting interest arrears.

The much-acclaimed economic turnaround in Latin America has produced little sign of recovery in per capita incomes. In 1990 per capita income fell for the third year in a row, leaving it at 10 percent below 1980's level though this aggregate conceals individual improvements in countries like Costa Rica, Colombia, and El Salvador (World Bank 1991, 133).

Nor is it likely that restructuring in its diverse dimensions will be able completely to redress the asymmetrical relationships between the United States and the rest of the hemisphere — both Canada in the North and Latin America in the South. The United States remains by far the dominant economic and military power in the region. This dominance affects different countries in different ways, and it is perhaps less pervasive further South, for example, in the countries of the Southern Common Market (MERCOSUR). It is a unique phenomenon and is not experienced to the same degree by any of the other emerging regional groupings (for example, in Europe or in the Asia-Pacific area).

A Western Hemisphere Community Model

The scope for mitigating this imbalance will depend, in part, on the approach adopted for the evolution of hemispheric development. Broadly speaking, there are two competing visions or models raised in the debate. One is the unipolar, dominant power — or hegemonic model — which is strongly influenced by the United States and is sometimes referred to as the "Washington consensus." In the trade literature, this is represented by the "hub and spoke" approach (Wonnacott 1990). Accordingly, the United States negotiates a series of bilateral free trade agreements, giving itself an advantage over all other countries as a location for investment (being the only country with free access to all markets in the hemisphere). Within this approach, the United States also has a bargaining advantage in bilateral negotiations as opposed to situations of plurilateral trade negotiation.

The second model is the pluralistic community or non-hegemonic model. In trade situations, this would lead to the negotiation of a plurilateral, hemispheric trade agreement, with all countries helping to design the rules and settle disputes and with all countries sharing in the economic opportunities of trade and investment liberalization. The hypothesis here is that it is in the interest of all countries to search for new partnerships to replace past conflictual and unstable relationships with the United States, and sometimes with each other, as well as the rather limited links with Canada.

Construction of this second model may not be easy. There will inevitably be tensions, even between Canada and Latin America. For example, as Stephen Blank and Leonard Waverman point out, dilution of the Canada-U.S. Free Trade Agreement (CUSFTA) brings with it not only the possibility of trade diversion but also the probability that outstanding bilateral (Canada-U.S.) differences, such as acceptable subsidy practice or the harmonization of environmental policies, may be increasingly difficult to resolve as more and more countries become involved in the negotiations. In terms of debt policy, Canada has maintained a position similar to that of the United States and other leading industrial nations in that it is reluctant to cancel official or multilateral debt and is keen to protect its own banks' interests (Culpeper 1992).

The parameters and limits of this Western Hemisphere Community model are pursued further in the following papers. Parameters include the extent to which it benefits all countries in the hemisphere; what shape the model might take and what institutional mechanisms are needed; and whether in some cases hemispheric disputes might best be resolved in a more global context (for example, within multilateral organizations such as the General Agreement on Tariffs and Trade — GATT).

What Role for the State?

A major subject in the debate about the evolution of the hemisphere, and a key theme addressed here, is the role of the State. Within Latin America, recent economic reform in most countries has involved extensive privatization. Fiscal constraints and doubt about the efficacy of government intervention have led to declining budgetary support for economic activity and for social and other government programs.

It is argued by Blank, Waverman, and other Western Hemisphere specialists that in many cases the private sector has led the government toward economic integration. States merely follow, for instance, in enacting trade agreements to formalize or institutionalize new forms of economic relationships. This parallels the process in the European Community (EC) which has an ever-expanding set of common market rules, but it is in sharp contrast to the East Asia trade framework, which remains controlled by the private sector rather than institutionalized by a set of formal intergovernmental agreements.

Such an approach may be inadequate in the Western Hemisphere for several reasons. One is that the development of a more cooperative model may require greater concerted leadership by governments, particularly Latin American and Canadian.

A second reason is that there are several important areas where the market has generally played a limited role. Canadian commercial linkages with Latin America typically have been weak and appear to require some catalytic involvement by the State. For example, two-way trade remained modest at $6.1 billion in 1989, which was less than 2 percent of total Canadian exports. Excluding the United States, the rest of the hemisphere only accounted for 6 percent of Canada's trade (less than the 6.5 percent accounted for by Korea and China together). Even before the debt crisis, Canada's exports to Latin America never accounted for more than 5 percent compared to the peak of 27 percent reached by U.S. exports. Most Canadian trade has been directed toward Mexico and Brazil, although recently trade has grown rapidly with Chile.

Elements of a Western Hemisphere Community Model: A Canadian Perspective

Several papers in this volume present a Canadian perspective on the following key elements of a Western Hemisphere model:

Competitiveness

One of the principal objectives of pursuing hemispheric integration is economic. The goal is to establish a regional base able to compete with producers in the other major production zones in Europe and the Asia-Pacific region. The process has already begun and is symbolized by the CUSFTA, the North American Free Trade Agreement (NAFTA), the Andean Pact, MERCOSUR, the Caribbean Common Market (CARICOM), and the set of framework agreements with the United States stemming from the Enterprise for the Americas Initiative (EAI). As a result, there now exists a complex hemispheric web of trade and investment agreements.

A major issue is whether Canadian-U.S. economic integration will guarantee that Canada also becomes more integrated with Mexico and countries further south. Market forces (primarily, the desire to compete with Asian, U.S., and other firms) have led several Canadian businesses to rationalize on a continental scope. Rationalization may extend on a hemisphere-wide basis should integration continue. However, it has been argued that U.S. integration with the Caribbean has led to increasing Canadian marginalization in that region.[1]

A major challenge for the countries in the Western Hemisphere will be the development of a set of rules and complementary policies that maximize the benefits of economic integration, including trade creation, while minimizing trade diversion — both on a hemispheric and global basis. The process must be outward- rather than inward-looking.

Social Policy

It is important for many Canadians that the process of economic rationalization recognizes certain social objectives leading to an upward rather than downward harmonization of social standards, including wages, health care, and the environment. The issue is whether integration will improve social standards or whether some government action will be necessary in the form of rules or financial adjustment assistance in order for tighter hemispheric economic linkages to be politically sustainable.

Canadian dissatisfaction with the government's handling of social policies and concern that the social "contract" radically rewritten by a series of policy changes including budgetary cuts have led to the suggestion that a Social Charter be incorporated in the Constitution (Echenberg 1992). A key objective of this Charter is to ensure that the State pays due attention to the social implications of its economic policies.

In Latin America severe fiscal constraints continue to limit many health, education, and social safety net programs, which hinder efforts to ease the process of adjustment. While it is generally accepted that structural change and economic growth must have "a human face" — that is, be socially acceptable, for example, avoiding the discontent witnessed recently in Venezuela — there is no consensus on structural adjustment assistance. Specifically, there is no consensus about the types and levels of support that are appropriate and how they should be funded.

Many non-governmental organizations (NGOs) in Canada, the United States, and Mexico have insisted that a social clause or charter be included in NAFTA and subsequent trade negotiations. How can governments, NGOs, or others in the private sector best help to raise social standards throughout the hemisphere? Would a regional assistance fund similar to that in the EC be an essential component? Some Canadian aid programs to Latin America and the Caribbean may provide useful examples, particularly the 18 percent of bilateral aid now delivered by several hundred Canadian NGOs, many of which are attempting to address the social consequences of economic adjustment.[2] Some of these themes are addressed by Laura Macdonald in her chapter on the changing role of Canadian NGOs, their engagement in the policy debate, and their social programs.

Migration

Without substantial progress toward reducing social inequities, there will continue to be migration of populations from South to North America. The main target for Latin American and Caribbean migrants has been the United States. Nonetheless, Alan Simmons' essay documents that this region accounts for approximately 15 percent of all immigrants to Canada. Most Latin American immigrants to Canada have been refugees primarily from Chile, El Salvador, and Argentina.

In particular, the Caribbean offers an interesting illustration of the complexities of migration, including the many factors driving migration (the push of economic, social, and security factors as well as the pull of established communities in Canada and the United States) and the wide range of policy responses in both host and home countries. Gregory Mahler elaborates on the consequences of these links for Canada's aid and commercial ties with the Caribbean.

Within the context of a hemispheric trade agreement, migration can be dealt with only partially in that trade may substitute for migration and that an agreement may cover labor or professional services requiring temporary population shifts. There is a need for new regional mechanisms to manage migration flows on a more humane and long-term basis rather than present ad hoc, national reactive policies. Canada's involvement in the design and implementation of this type of arrangement is one of the topics addressed by Alan Simmons.

Governance

Before embarking on the development of a new hemispheric

model, it is important to take stock of the evolution of the existing set of regional institutions and Canada's role in them. As Stephen Randall's contribution aptly demonstrates, there is a long history of Canadian involvement in these institutions, though overshadowed until the late 1960s by a focus on other regions (in particular, Europe) and Canadian reticence to interfere in the U.S. sphere of influence. The 1970 White Paper on foreign policy signalled the beginning of a new era in Canada-Latin America relations, a point emphasized by Gordon Mace.

In addition, Canada's experience in using the CUSFTA and other bilateral or plurilateral mechanisms to resolve disputes with the United States could be of interest to Latin America. Canada's economic strength is large relative to many other countries in the hemisphere. As such, it may be able to assist with collaborative bargaining on trade and other topics with the United States.

A number of the questions already raised about the role of government and the need for leadership are relevant here. At the intergovernmental level, the prospect of an endless series of criss-crossing trade agreements raises the issue of the appropriate forum for promoting Canada-Latin America linkages. Could a single plurilateral mechanism not suffice? This is a variation on the "hub and spoke" theme raised by Wonnacott (1990). Are we risking what has been called "institutional overcrowding" (Mortimer 1992)?

Multiple Sovereignties

Difficulties in designing a new hemispheric model arise with the emergence of competing responsibilities between different levels of government.

What is the appropriate division of powers among these groups? Traditionally, trade has been considered to be the domain of the federal government. However, trade has increasingly involved the discussion of industrial, agricultural, financial services, or investment policies that are the responsibility of provinces or states. Canadian provinces clearly feel that closer federal-provincial consultation is in order, a fact reflecting their different priorities. British Columbia's closer links to the Pacific Rim than to Ontario exemplify that different provinces have diverse trade interests.[3]

Some of these complexities are raised by Blank and Waverman, while Mace elaborates on Quebec's relations with Latin America and their interplay with federal activities in the region. This is not only an issue of trade and scientific cooperation. It also extends to cultural and immigration policies that are the subject of an ongoing Canadian debate about the devolution of powers to the provinces.

Cultural Sustainability

A serious governance issue common to many countries in the hemisphere, and one which has been highlighted in the ensuing Canadian constitutional debate, is the treatment of first nations or aboriginal peoples. In Canada and other countries of the Americas, recognition of this cultural diversity, in its broadest sense, is an urgent priority. Greater sensitivity toward traditional values and the distribution of wealth among the entire population is needed in the design of new approaches to development. It is important not just for the aboriginal peoples themselves but also for the stability and progress of our societies as a whole.

Entrenching the inherent right to self-government will affect policies ranging from economic to social, legal, and environmental. Frances Abele's essay raises related issues under discussion in Canada, such as the relationship of individuals to collective rights, comprehensive claims agreements, and the devolution of program responsibilities to aboriginal collectives. These could provide important lessons for other countries in the hemisphere.

Security, Democracy, and Human Rights

Finally, for many Canadians a key test of the success of any new hemispheric arrangement will be whether it is able to sustain and strengthen recent fragile improvements in security, democracy, and human rights in the region.

Traditionally, Canada has been seen as lacking active interest in hemispheric security questions. For example, the Trilateral Commission report notes Canada's decision not to join the Inter-American Defense Board, when it assumed full membership in the Organization of American States (OAS). In sharp contrast to the United States, it does not provide security assistance to the region. On the other hand, Canada has provided support to peacekeeping efforts in Nicaragua and

El Salvador, helped to train some police forces in the Caribbean, and pressed for an end to human rights abuses. More recently, Canada, together with other OAS members, was actively involved in attempting to shore up democracy in Haiti.

Given that direct military takeovers are no longer as pervasive a threat to democratic and economic progress in Latin America as before,[4] a new definition of security is needed. What is necessary is one that addresses broader political, governance, and economic factors rather than just focusing on military/strategic dimensions. These issues are pursued in the chapter by Hal Klepak.

Improvements in regional security will depend on the success of economic and political reforms as well as on strategic factors. As James Rochlin suggests, attempts to end the narcotics trade are unlikely to prove successful if drug trafficking is treated primarily as a security issue warranting a military response rather than one requiring anti-poverty policies, land redistribution, and political reforms in producing countries as well as measures to reduce demand for drugs in consumer countries.

Likewise, strengthening democracy and respect for human rights must be central in any new hemispheric model. It is no longer acceptable or effective to deal with these issues separately from trade or other economic relations such as aid or investment. This is not to suggest that sanctions are the solution. Positive measures are needed, including assistance in strengthening civil society institutions, for example, following the approach of Canada's recently established International Center for Human Rights and Democratic Development.

Questions remain about the appropriate international forums for addressing these topics. There has been a revival of global interest in the United Nations, partly triggered by its role in the 1991 Gulf War as well as by its efforts to promote peaceful resolution of conflicts in El Salvador, Yugoslavia, and Cambodia. There are arguments for and against using an intra-regional body, such as the OAS, to resolve regional security issues, such as strategic planning and narcotics trafficking, rather than bilateral or multilateral alternatives.

Conclusion

The following chapters address a rich and wide-ranging set of issues relevant to the debate about the future role of Canada in the Americas. They are not comprehensive — a notable exclusion is discussion of environmental management — nor are they exhaustive. Several of the papers identify areas for further research. Rather, they serve to launch a process of research and debate about a new Western Hemisphere Community Model to be continued during the next several years.

Notes

[1] "The rhetoric, if not the accomplishments, of the Caribbean Basin Initiative (CBI), has pushed the interest in Canadian business and markets to the margin." Redma Consultants, 1991, "Likely Economic Impact of the NAFTA on Prospects for Caribbean Exports to Canada," mimeo (November), 9.

[2] For example, programs in Jamaica, Guyana, Costa Rica, Honduras, Nicaragua, Bolivia, Uruguay, and Peru according to the Canadian International Development Agency, 1992-93, *Estimates Part III*, 92-93.

[3] Japan alone accounted for $5.1 billion of British Columbia's exports in 1989, compared to the $7.2 billion exported to the United States. For Ontario, corresponding figures were $822 million and $56.1 billion.

[4] See *The Americas in a New World, The 1990 Report of the Inter-American Dialogue*, 1990 (Washington, D.C.: The Aspen Institute).

References

Canadian International Development Agency. 1992. *Estimates Part III 1992-93*. Ottawa: Canadian International Development Agency.

Clark, The Hon. J. 1990. "Canadian Policy Towards Latin America." Speech delivered in Calgary, February.

Culpeper, Roy. 1992. "The Great Debt Crisis of the 1990s. Treating the Casualties, Preventing the Next Outbreak." *North-South Institute*, Ottawa (March).

Echenberg, Havi, et al. 1992. *A Social Charter for Canada? Perspective on the Constitutional Entrenchment of Social Rights*. Toronto: C.D. Howe Institute.

Inter-American Dialogue. 1990. *The Americas in a New World*. Washington, D.C.: The Aspen Institute.

Landau, George, et al. 1990. *Latin America at the Crossroads: The Challenge to the Trilateral Countries: Triangle Papers 39*. New York: Trilateral Commission (August).

Mortimer, Edward. 1992. "Europe's Security Surplus." *Financial Times*. March 3.

Redma Consultants. 1991. "Likely Economic Impact of the NAFTA on Prospects for Caribbean Exports to Canada." Mimeo, November.

Wonnacott, Ronald. 1990. *U.S. Hub-and-Spoke Bilateral and the Multilateral Trading System: C.D. Howe Institute Commentary 23*. Toronto: C.D. Howe Institute (October).

World Bank. 1991. *Annual Report*. Washington, D.C.: Oxford University Press.

Chapter I

THE CHANGING INFRASTRUCTURE OF NORTH AMERICA AND ITS IMPACT ON CANADA'S RELATIONS WITH LATIN AMERICA

Stephen Blank and Leonard Waverman

Introduction

This paper seeks to accomplish two objectives. One is to provide an overview of Canadian economic interests and policies in Latin America and the Caribbean. The second is to position this in the context of the changing structure of the North American economic, political, legal, and corporate systems and to try to discern implications for future relationships in the hemisphere.

In the context of an evolving North American economic system, we need to look at hemispheric relations through a new optic. To grasp the nature and impact of these changes, we need not only data but also new conceptual lenses to help us look at what are basically familiar phenomena from a new perspective. Let us suggest several examples of what we mean by new conceptual lenses. For more than a decade, we have been aware of the erosion of higher value-added blue collar (and, more recently, white collar) jobs in the face of new technology. However, we have also continued to assume that employment would inevitably track the business cycle. We are now facing the realization

Support from the University of Miami North-South Center for both authors and from the Ontario Centre for International Business for Dr. Waverman is gratefully acknowledged.

Stephen Blank is with the Americas Society in New York; Leonard Waverman is with the Centre for International Studies in Toronto.

1

that this is not the case and that the long-term, perhaps permanent, unemployment of large numbers of formerly higher value-added manufacturing and service workers will be a key economic, social, and political issue for the future.

Similarly, we have long assumed that lower trade barriers would lead to global economic integration. We have learned, however, that the reduction of water's edge trade barriers may actually lead to new conflicts as trade and investment flows come to be shaped more by domestic policies and structures. It was easier to negotiate tariff reductions than to deal with the trade impact of domestic subsidies, of social programs, or of industrial structure.

Canada's role in Latin America and the Caribbean (LAC) and the nature of the basic trade and investment relationships in an evolving Western Hemisphere Free Trade Association (WHFTA) between Canada and LAC require serious and deep analyses. This paper is a beginning to this required study.

Canada and Canadian Trade Policy in Latin America and the Caribbean

Canada sits at the northern end of North America, and its trade, investment, and political relations are concentrated on the United States. Nearly three-quarters of Canadian trade is with the United States, whereas Latin America and the Caribbean account for less than 5 percent, a third of which is with Mexico. Similarly, the United States is the predominant market for the rest of the hemisphere, absorbing over 40 percent of its exports. Investment patterns are also asymmetric. Canadian private foreign investment in LAC is not insubstantial ($8 billion in 1989).[1] Nevertheless, the bulk of investment in that region originates in the United States. Furthermore, the United States has, itself, been the major foreign location for Canadian investors (totalling $50 billion in 1989).

Until the late 1970s, Canada's national industrial policy involved fairly high effective tariff and non-tariff barriers amid an array of other federal government policies designed to increase industrial output and reduce dependence on the export of semi- or unprocessed natural resource products.[2] Trade strategy up to the early 1980s could still be summarized as "mainly multilateralist." For a smaller nation heavily dependent on trade, the GATT offered an effective means to prevent its larger trading partners (especially the United States) from introducing unilateral trade restrictions. At the same time, it offered a means to reduce dependence on the U.S. market by promoting trade with third countries. But the emerging realization of the extent of economic integration in North America, together with growing concerns about U.S. protectionism and Washington's apparent resistance to dealing in the GATT, led Canada to move bilaterally.

Since the mid-1980s, the Conservative federal government, in keeping with its non-interventionist ideology and its attempt to reduce the fiscal deficit, has introduced a series of radical changes. A range of trade, industrial, and regional assistance programs, which had been considered by some to be a failure,[3] have gradually been cut back.[4]

The CUSFTA was seen as essential to promote rationalization of Canadian industry and to increase productivity through the achievement of economies of scale, permitted by more secure access to the large U.S. market.

The third, and still ongoing, phase of Canadian trade strategy can be characterized as one of "reluctant regionalism." Canada has been involved in several loose regional initiatives, such as the Pacific Basin Economic Cooperation, on the understanding that this should not undermine multilateralism: The benefits negotiated in such arrangements were open to other members, and Canada continued to be a strong supporter of the GATT.

The suggestion in early 1990 of a free trade agreement between the United States and Mexico took many in Canada, including the federal and provincial governments, by surprise. Thus, the strategy that has been adopted is defensive and reactive. Canada would probably not have sought a free trade agreement with Mexico if the United States had not done so, nor would it have become involved in free trade discussions with Latin America and the Caribbean in the absence of the U.S. Enterprise for the Americas Initiative (EAI).[5] Although renewed Canadian interest in the region dates from an earlier 1988 cabinet review which led to various Canadian initiatives — notably, full membership in the Organization of American States in 1990 — the cabinet has yet to approve the move from a framework of regional trade, investment and/ or tax accords to a full-fledged free trade agreement.

A chief reason for Canada's participation in the NAFTA negotiations is to ensure that Canada offers investors (of any country) the same advantage of free access to all three markets as does the United States.

If the United States negotiates a series of bilateral free trade agreements with other countries of the region, a "hub and spoke" trading system could emerge in which the United States, as the "hub," would have an advantage over any one of the "spokes" (Lipsey 1990; Wonnacott 1990). Another important reason is to try to protect Canada's recently acquired interests in the U.S. market through involvement in the negotiations on the auto sector, rules of origin, and the phasing in of liberalization. Several studies have underlined the risks of some trade diversion away from Canada due to the possible overlap between Mexican and Canadian products.

With respect to the EAI, Canada already offers preferential trade with several countries in the Caribbean and has wider bilateral aid interests in many parts of the region.

Latin America and the Caribbean represent a market of 445 million people (1990 data) and $820 billion in gross regional product (1989). In 1989 the total imports of LAC were $115 billion (a little below the level of Canadian imports). As growth resumes in LAC and the debt crisis subsides, imports will increase enormously, having tumbled by a dramatic 40 percent from 1980 to 1989. Liberalized trade in the Western Hemisphere would then offer an important advantage to Canada, the opportunities resulting from trade and investment preferences in this huge market.[6] Nevertheless, there are also several disadvantages that may result, including increased competition from LAC producers in U.S. and Canadian markets and potential conflicts over appropriate trade policies for subsidies, innovation, and trade-related investment measures (TRIMS). Given Canada's minuscule exports to LAC, trade creation would depend on a focused attempt by Canadian entrepreneurs to tap this growing market.

Data for 1991 show that Canada has not yet benefited from such trade creation with Mexico; in fact, Canadian exports to Mexico fell from their 1990 level while imports from Mexico rose.[7] Canada's direct investment in Mexico is also minimal; new Canadian investment in Mexico may be a necessary precursor to greater Canadian exports.

Canada, long a leading advocate of multilateralism and the GATT, realizes that multilateralism provides important benefits to small countries. Though many Canadian nationalists decry the loss of Canadian sovereignty implicit in CUSFTA, they tend to ignore what could be a greater loss of U.S. sovereignty. A multilateral institution whose decision-making mechanisms are autonomous and rules-based can, as long as the rules are neutral, lead to a much greater *relative* loss of power for the stronger partner(s).

The current tensions between Canada and the United States reflect the fact that in a bilateral rules-based institution, attention is focused on the one other party, with the risk that the rules will not, in fact, remain neutral. Hence, Canada's long-standing preference for multilateral institutions: such institutions diffuse the attention of the powerful member. In addition, the plurality of voices and decision-making procedures based on one vote per country rather than on power relationships tends to favor small countries.[8] Thus, Canada could be better off in a Western Hemispheric free trade area where rules-based institutions are maintained by the decisions of many countries.

The Erosion of the State-Centered System and the Rise of a New Architecture of North America

The relationship between Canada and LAC also reflects and is structured by dramatic changes taking place in the nature of the North American economic, political, legal, and corporate systems.

The period from the late nineteenth century to the late twentieth century was unified primarily by technology, a system of production that began with the technological improvements in energy, transportation, and communications, which are typically terms of the "Second Industrial Revolution."[9] It was a period unified by social patterns as well, dominated by the factory system and standardized mass production, by urbanization and the creation of enormous city-centers of production and exchange, and by social systems centered on class. Finally, it was a period unified by political patterns — of the nation state. It was in this period that state-centered economic and trade policies were fashioned, including tariffs, subsidies, and protection of markets.

Today, the world is changing around us in profound and uncertain ways. First is a vast change in how things are made in the dominant "production paradigm," which has enormous impact on our entire economic system. This "Third Industrial Revolution" is driven by new technology, hinging on computerization and automation capacities, by much more flexible production systems, and by smaller optimum production runs. It undermines the competitive advantage of standardization and economies of scale that structured industrial systems markets and government economics and trade for the past century.

Social and political implications are crucial. Most important is a dramatic change in the role of labor, with a critical loss of blue collar employment and of the social system that surrounded the urban/factory/union system. The conflict between this erosion and events integrating the lower-wage LAC with North America is clear.

Another structural change in this emerging environment is the diminished capacity of central governments to manage formerly national economies and to guarantee national prosperity. The state as it emerged in the post-World War II era, in which most social systems (not only law and force, but education, social welfare, industrial development, research and development, and the economy itself) came to be defined in national terms, is breaking down. This has resulted in an "unbundling" of social systems from state control.

Few would disagree with the statement that the United States and Canada are "sovereign" states. But these two sovereign states increasingly share a single economy. Thus, sovereignty must be redefined to encourage — and not undermine — economic welfare. The CUSFTA is a small step in this direction — principally, in binational dispute resolution — but it does not address crucial aspects of the relationship, namely, domestic policies that aid, assist, or impede trade and foreign direct investment (FDI).

Ohmae-Porter:
The Relationship Between States and Markets

Kenichi Ohmae, Michael Porter, and strategic trade theorists such as Paul Krugman have differing views about the emerging relationship between states and markets. It is not yet clear what roles governments can best provide.

Ohmae's view is that consumer consciousness, expanded by economic development, simply explodes the boundaries of the state: "The role of national governments is much less important than they think.... Governments are little more than spoilers who disrupt markets with their interference and announcements" (1990). For Ohmae (1990a) a global company must free itself from the domination of its parent headquarters. In each major market, it strives to be an "insider," tailoring products to local tastes and standards. This is a marketing prospective and focuses on global consumption and access to products.

Michael Porter (1990), on the other hand, begins at the production end of the process. He says that conditions in a company's home country — "clusters of excellence" — are crucial to its competitiveness abroad. Furthermore, competitiveness is viewed by Porter as a function of clusters: "rivals, their suppliers, related industries, and sophisticated customers in close proximity create a rapid rate of progress" (1990b).

From yet another point of view, strategic trade theorists view the state as not only providing an environment for firms to enhance international competitive advantage but also as a direct source of innovation. The state can "manipulate" competitive advantage by funding research and development (R&D), by developing education and infrastructure, and by encouraging close cooperation with national firms.

These views focus on the role of the state in creating and enhancing competitive advantage. Porter sees establishing conditions for intense competition among national firms as critical toward shaping international competitiveness, while the strategic trade theorists place more weight on cooperation between government and national firms. Porter, nevertheless, still underlines the central role of the "state": "Globalization does not supersede the role of states and of domestic competition but arguably makes them even more important. National differences in values, institutions, and culture are integral to innovation" (1990a).

This debate will surely continue within the context of the technological, economic, social, and political revolutions we have described. It is crucial to realize that competitiveness in the emerging global economy remains, at least in part, a function of the state. One company standing alone is unlikely to be highly competitive globally, and international competitiveness is achieved more often by groups of national firms based on their relationships with one another in the context of a particular national environment and policies. The addition of LAC to the CUSFTA will not only create new competition (trade diversion) but will also affect the ability of traditional clusters to continue. For example, will Canadian firms learn to out-source as Japanese firms have?

Linked Loyalties and Pooled Sovereignties

A much more complex system of *linked loyalties* and linked or *pooled sovereignties* has emerged to replace the simple state system. We can see this development in Europe, and it is beginning in North America in the Great Lakes Region with the Red River Consortium (Minnesota, North Dakota, Manitoba) and with the collaboration between British Columbia and the state of Washington. The new Pacific Northwest Economic Region (PNWER*) also increased trade links between Quebec and New York. Therefore, instead of a single political entity, it is likely that in the future we will live as members of several different but overlapping political systems. We will identify with each of these systems, and each will draw to some degree upon our loyalty. This is what is meant by *linked loyalty.*

For example, the CUSFTA acknowledged a certain basic reality; while we remain citizens of two separate, independent countries, we also share a common economy. The boundary of the economy in North America is no longer the same as the political boundaries of our two countries. Our nations are sovereign, but the operations of the continental economy and the rules of dispute resolution, for example, overlay and limit those sovereignties. This what we mean by *pooled sovereignty.*

We are separately Canadians and citizens of the United States, but we are also North Americans. In many contexts, our identity as Canadians may be much more important than any other. However, in other contexts, such as multilateral trade negotiations or in negotiations with the EC or with Japanese car manufacturers, our identity as North Americans may be more important.

Clearly, identities are not only emerging upward — toward larger groupings of states — but also "downward," with the growing importance of regional loyalties and identities. Cases such as the emerging identities within the former Soviet Union and Eastern Europe have been growing in Canada and in the United States as well. William Wallace (1990) writes about the emerging Europe and has caught the sense of this complexity well:

> The emergence of a diffuse sense of European identity has *not* led to a transfer of loyalties from the national to the European level, as some foresaw. What we have observed across Western Europe over the last two decades is a shift toward multiple loyalties, with the single focus on the nation supplemented by European and regional affiliations above and below.

The Pacific Northwest Economic Region embraces three Canadian provinces (Alberta, British Columbia, and Saskatchewan) and five U.S. states (California, Idaho, Montana, Oregon, and Washington).

French and Germans now also share, to some degree, a sense of European identity, which allows EC institutions to have a continuing substantial impact on their lives. Regional identities are also major elements in the new political, economic, social, and psychological map. Scots, Bavarians, and Northern Italians, for example, increasingly view themselves as appropriate entities for carrying out certain political or economic functions.

The outlines of these emerging systems are vague. Regionality and ethnicity may reinforce one another, or they may compete with each other. Powers and responsibilities are being shifted upward and downward, sometimes formally, sometimes only functionally.

We are not moving toward Ohmae's "borderless" world but rather toward a world of many overlapping borders and many political authorities which increasingly share functions. Quebec provides for many of its inhabitants a primary cultural and linguistic identity. Yet few Quebeckers would not acknowledge that they form part of a wider Quebec-Ontario-New York State-New England economic region. Rules must, therefore, be laid out to facilitate regional economic progress and welfare. In addition, the rules must attempt to ensure that the fundamental values which they share with other Canadians are reinforced, while other social systems and rules can best be organized by this regional entity. Finally, vis-à-vis Japan or Europe, Quebeckers may feel a sort of North American identity and acknowledge the need for structures that will support North American economic development for such areas as automobiles and high-tech industries.

Changing North American Political, Economic, and Legal Systems

In this view, the CUSFTA was not the beginning of a process of economic integration between the United States and Canada. Rather, the free trade agreement (FTA) marked the recognition by both sides of the high levels of integration and rapidly growing interdependence that already existed. The FTA rested on the need to develop new rules and practices that would lessen the danger that unilateral actions by either side would jeopardize this new situation. The CUSFTA should, therefore, be viewed as one of several emerging responses to this dynamic that encompass the following changes.

Political Change

An important aspect of political change is the eroding power of central governments in both countries. Both Canada and the United States have central governments with an ability to protect regions in the country from the impact of changes in international price movements. In both countries, changes in the federal system are shifting many new responsibilities and powers to states and provinces. Both countries face a wide array of institutional frictions. U.S. state governments, for example, are not well-structured to bear the kind of heavy policy and fiscal responsibilities they now confront. In Canada there is a growing criticism of central governmental institutions and demands for institutional reform.

Yet, at the same time, there are demands for the reaffirmation of "national symbols" and values along with increasing concerns about threats to cultural identity or political autonomy in the face of growing foreign or "global" presence in domestic economies.

Economic Change

One vital change in the structure of our economies is the growing influence of regions within nations and regions crossing national borders. From a high point of the centralization of economic policy and direction in both countries in the 1970s, we have seen a remarkable decentralization of economic power and authority in our two countries. The rising flow of goods, services, and investment across increasingly open borders has not increased evenly. As international flows deepen in certain areas, new interests are created, and new distances emerge within nations.

About 40 percent of all U.S. exports to Japan, for example, originate in three states — California, Washington, and Oregon. It is clear that the interests of these states are going to be substantially shaped by this deepening Pacific relationship. One economist writes that in California hundreds of millions of dollars in special industrial tax credits that can be traded among Californian, Japanese, Malaysian, Singaporean, and other Pacific Rim companies have been issued in coordination with Japan's Ministry of Finance. A consortium of private California banks, backed by the Japanese Ministry of Finance, offers risk-calibrated deposit insurance for their largest depositors, and an increasingly large number of accounts there are now denominated in yen. "It's not that California has become any less a part of the United States," the author observes, "it's just that the state has also become a more explicit part of the Pacific Rim" (Schrage 1990).

Other economic changes include the increasing diversity of fiscal and policy mixes among U.S. states and Canadian provinces; heightened competition among states and provinces for foreign investment; and the emergence of important new state-level industrial strategies, here following Canadian practice.

What these developments suggest, following Michael Porter's notion of "clusters of excellence," is that such clusters are more likely to develop for most industrial sectors at regional and local rather than national levels. As such, we are likely to see the emergence of a North American economic geography characterized by increasing specialization and competition among sub-national and cross-border regions.

Legal Change

Allan E. Gotlieb, former Canadian ambassador to the United States and a well-known legal scholar, described "international law in a North American economic space" as an emerging legal environment in which the integration of economies rendered international law in its traditional sense relatively irrelevant.[10] Relations between the two countries are increasingly shaped not by arm's length or water's edge laws and regulations but by domestic policies. Increasingly, domestic regulations and practices shape trade and investment flows as well as competitive advantage.

Economic integration gives rise to an increasing number of regulatory incongruities. For example, while it might well be deemed good business practice for an American power producer, such as the Bonneville Power Authority, to offer deep discounts to its corporate customers, it is viewed as a violation of trade law if a Canadian producer, such as Hydro-Quebec, provides a similar discount to its customers who trade with American clients. If we have free trade, Canadians argue, traditional regulatory definitions based on national sovereignty need to be revised. The same rules should apply to Hydro-Quebec as to an American power authority when they are dealing in the same markets.

Gotlieb speaks of the emergence of a "new jurisprudence," the beginnings of which are already visible in the Canada-U.S. dispute settlement process, which builds on the domestic legal structures of the two nations but constitutes a substantially new addition to the legal system. Additionally, Gotlieb sees the emergence of a tri-level legal and political structure in North America: an over-arching North American framework, national systems, and strong regional systems within this. In his view, a key issue over the foreseeable future will almost surely be competition among regulatory authorities for control over particular environments.

Impact on Firms

Firms, particularly in the United States, are evolving new strategies and structures for North American markets since they can no longer operate small Canadian branches sheltered behind high Canadian tariffs. A more open Canadian economy forces firms to restructure their Canadian operations within the context of continental or regional interests.

The constant fire of criticism that American firms are "abandoning" Canada misses the point. In fact, what we see in many cases are new corporate organizational structures and strategies. These raise a whole array of questions dealing with maintaining sensitivities to cultural, linguistic, and political differences out of a common structure.

What Does All This Mean for Canada and the EAI?

LAC and the Erosion of State-Centered Systems

How does EAI fit with the earlier arguments about the erosion of state-centered systems? CUSFTA represents the recognition by central governments of the reality of corporate-led, Canada-U.S. economic integration. However, it is the national governments that make international agreements, negotiate trade pacts, set tariffs, and initiate countervailing duties and anti-dump actions. Thus, the notion of linked loyalties and pooled sovereignties has implications for the setting of trade policy.

Clearly, regional interests in LAC and the United States see benefits from closer integration. There may be interests that see gains from closer ties between Canada and the Caribbean. There are no shared borders, no contiguous regions between Canada and LAC in the traditional sense, and, therefore, geographic "gravity"-type models that explain a lot of trade on the basis of geographic closeness do not seem relevant here.

However, it is important to recognize that Monterrey, Mexico, is about the same distance from Toronto as Edmonton is. Finance, trade, and investment create new linkages, even without contiguous borders, and Canada will be increasingly linked to LAC. While the Canadian federal government appears to act as leader — and a trade pact will precede integration — business ties and trade flows will determine Canada's "borders."

The Ohmae/Porter/Krugman controversies on the role of borders and states point out important aspects of a Western Hemisphere Free Trade Agreement (WHFTA). The Ohmae view, from a neoclassical economics perspective, would see the comparative advantage of home-based multinational companies (MNCs) from Canada, the United States, Mexico, or each LAC country leading these MNCs to compete by expanding through the Western Hemisphere (WH) and increasing the product differentiation available to consumers. The Porter view would see new clusters in the WH through a reshaping of tasks. Thus, job functions would move so as to improve efficiency.

James Womack (1990) says NAFTA will improve the competitiveness of traditional North American automobile companies by shifting small car assembly and some component production from Asia to Mexico. Thus, formal integration improves the efficiency of existing clusters. A Krugman-type story would incorporate an analysis of how competition changes when barriers are removed. The important, yet unanswered, question is how EAI will affect local and regional clusters in Canada and in the United States.

Thus, we are in a period of profound change. The impacts of a WHFTA on the political, economic, corporate, labor, and social organization of Canada and the United States require serious analytical study. The impetus will be deep and strong and will reorganize economic, political, and legal ties.

Economics

In 1990 LAC absorbed 14 percent of U.S. exports, more than Japan and the East Asian newly industrializing countries (NICs), with Mexico accounting for approximately one half. Latin America is a particularly important buyer of U.S. machinery and transportation equipment, whereas U.S. imports from LAC are heavily petroleum — 25 percent of all U.S. purchases in the region. LAC is host for 16 percent of all U.S. FDI, more than Japan and the East Asian NICs combined. In fact, U.S. trade deficits since the early 1980s can be seen more as a result of the collapse of U.S. export markets in LAC — due to the impact of the debt crisis — than to the surge of imports from Japan. Indeed, if U.S.-LAC export markets had held up through the 1980s, and the LAC countries had continued along even a moderate growth path, the Japanese "problem" might look much less urgent today. The Bush administration's EAI makes sense viewed from this perspective.

There is, however, almost no trade between Canada and LAC. Thus, Canadian interest in LAC must be defined, perhaps by utilizing existing investment flows predominant in the Caribbean as a way to extend it to the rest of LAC.[11] The potential economic costs include trade diversion in U.S. markets (a loss of Canadian exports), increased competition in Canadian markets, and, consequently, reduced investment and employment. Potential economic gains, on the other hand, involve preferential access for Canadian investment and exports to LAC, which, given the size of this market, could be substantial.

In 1988 Canada exported $1.9 billion to LAC (down from $2.8 billion in 1980), which is a tiny amount when compared to the $82 billion in exports to the United States. Similarly, Canada's imports from LAC are small — $2.8 billion in 1988. Mexico is Canada's single largest LAC trading partner and accounted for 29 percent of trade with LAC. Machinery, vehicles, chemicals, plastics, and miscellaneous manufacturing represent 42 percent of Canadian exports to LAC, and food products and wood products represent 39 percent. Whereas LAC accounted for a substantial 23 percent share of Canadian outward FDI in 1978, by 1988 this share had declined to 10 percent. Investment was concentrated in Brazil in the earlier period (60 percent) and has now shifted to the Bahamas and other Caribbean islands. Between 1978 and 1983, total Canadian FDI in the Latin American and Caribbean region was $2.8 billion; in 1988 it had risen to $7.3 billion.

Initially, Latin America attracted Canadian capital and entrepreneurs in search of low labor costs. However, in the late 1970s, there was a change of focus toward the East Asian NICs, which had low labor costs combined with more stable political and economic environments. As a result, the share of Canadian "developing-country" investment going to Latin America fell from a high of 88.1 percent in 1975 to a low of 57.7 percent in 1984.

Conspicuous for their lack of presence in the Canadian FDI picture are the larger Latin American countries. Mexico, for example, saw its share of the region's Canadian FDI increase from 2.1 percent in 1978 to 8.4 percent in 1984, but it declined again to 2.4 percent in 1988. Venezuela, with an average of only 1.7 percent over the eleven-year period and a high of only 2.8 percent, has never been a serious location for Canadian FDI. Likewise, Argentina figures much less prominently than its natural resource and agriculture-driven economy might suggest. Growing investment in the Bahamas and other Caribbean islands has not led to increased Canadian exports; thus, there does not appear to be a correlation between investment and trade.

While analysts concentrate on this cross-border data, Canadians must understand that the border around their country is not secure, that profound changes are under way, and that new associations are required.

Why Should Canada Be Interested in the Enterprise for the Americas Initiative?

The extent of economic gains and medium-term dislocations and costs from a WHFTA depends on the extent of trade and investment changes. There is not much information, data, or analysis upon which to base informed judgment. Markusen and Wigle (1990) argue that North-South trade will increase at a greater rate than North-North or South-South trade after liberalization because of existing barriers preventing South-North trade.

Others suggest that North-South trade will be largely unaffected by liberalization, and they raise the question of whether LAC-North America trade will follow traditional comparative advantage (interindustry) or product differentiation (intra-industry) patterns. Would a WHFTA cause LAC to specialize in labor- and resource-rich products, or is a NIC model applicable with a quick upgrading of skills and technology to produce differentiated manufacturing products? For

Canada, the type of trade that may develop after liberalization is an important determinant of detrimental trade diversion.

How do the Ohmae/Porter/Krugman interpretations see trade patterns developing? An Ohmae borderless world would see U.S. and Canadian firms expanding into production in LAC, perhaps to serve local markets. Additionally, it would allow for some exports, with minimal "head office" functions placed in LAC. Porter would examine existing and emerging clusters in LAC and North America to determine the potential for sustained product development, and strategic trade theorists would examine the nature of existing barriers and protection in LAC markets to determine the kinds of industrial responses possible.

Obviously, each of these "stories" sees different trade patterns emerging. How will Canadian and U.S. firms, as well as Association of Southeast Asian Nations (ASEAN) firms, respond? Will trade substitute for investment between North America and LAC, or will inward investment from North America have to lead trade? As noted above, Canadian investment in Mexico is small, and exports mirror this. Furthermore, both Canadian investment and trade with South America have been stagnant.

What should be the roles for central, regional, and local governments? What about NGOs? What rules on technology transfer are required before Northern Hemisphere to LAC investment occurs? The research agenda is vast and must include, we suggest, the new "optics" suggested in this paper.

Political and Social

There are potential political gains for Canada from EAI since multilateral trade agreements could, in general, provide more protection than a bilateral agreement with the United States. In multilateral trade negotiations, there are multiple votes diminishing the power of any one vote; thus, the United States could not exercise its weight proportionately in a multilateral framework. However, these potential benefits are tempered by the following uncertainties and constraints, all of which require analysis:

1. Are arrangements in CUSFTA, such as dispute resolution, so specific to a Canada-U.S. relationship that adding more players

diminishes the gains from this relationship?

2. Can two developed countries establish institutions and solutions to problems which will not be watered down when a number of less developed countries (LDCs) are added?

3. Are the basic notions of the role of the state so different between North America and LAC, that attempting to add LAC to the CUSFTA will produce severe problems in settling government procurement issues and defining subsidies?

4. There are substantive differences between North and South in the use and tradition of legal institutions. Will civil law-based systems, such as Mexico's or Chile's, be compatible with the common law systems in much of North America? Can the dispute resolution system in CUSFTA be applied to diverse legal regimes?

5. Will the addition of LAC reduce the incentives for binational discussions on environmental or social policy?

6. If, as suggested, pooled sovereignty and linked loyalties are the profound new forces shaping relationships in North America, how will adding LAC compound these forces? There are clear "linked" loyalties between peoples on both sides of the Rio Grande; however, Canada is not physically contiguous to LAC. Thus, will U.S. interests drift away from Canada toward LAC, and would this drift be good or bad?

7. Will the formation of a WHFTA accentuate regional identities within states — for example, the emergence of a Texas-California-Northern Mexico economic region or a Pacific Northwest Economic Region? If so, how will this affect North American political and economic structures?

8. Will linked loyalties and pooled sovereignty generate a new legal jurisprudence that will leave Canada on the outside? Will these trends in jurisprudence be disadvantageous to Canada?

9. What will be the impact of these western hemispheric developments on the multilateral trading system? Is there an inevitable trend toward the formation of blocs, or is it possible that a greater regional trade system will not lead to the formation of an inward-looking bloc?

10. What sets of transitional and structural policies should be put in place to ameliorate changes induced in Canada by EAI?

Firms

How firms will react to EAI is unclear and rests on the Ohmae/Porter/Krugman debates discussed earlier. This corporate reaction is clearly crucial when determining the costs and benefits to Canada resulting from EAI. Research is needed on an industry-by-industry basis to examine the changes in production, trade, and sourcing which would follow from a WHFTA. Key sectors include 1) autos and auto parts, 2) mining, 3) petroleum, 4) forestry products, 5) textiles and apparel, 6) high-tech, and 7) agriculture.

These sectors are major Canadian employers and are organized along very different lines. The automobile industry consists of large multinationals with Canadian-owned firms in the parts sector. Foreign firms are making inroads into the largely Canadian-owned forestry product industry that is also experiencing losses in traditional U.S. markets.

Textiles and apparel, as well as agriculture, are made up of many small firms. The structures of these industries vary, as does the source of their strengths, comparative advantages (for example, forestry), and scale economies and product differentiations. Since the extent of LAC strengths and structure also varies, forecasting change requires both a "traditional" economic analysis (an analysis of changing competitive conditions) and the use of new optics — an analysis of the changing "borders" to determine new organizations and new competition.

The Benefits to Latin America from Canadian Involvement in EAI[12]

There are, in turn, a number of potentially significant benefits to Latin America from Canada's involvement in EAI; the possible magnitude of these benefits belies the modest current level of economic and political interaction between Canada and LAC. In purely economic terms, Canada has special expertise in several industries of importance to LAC, and it has been an important source of direct investment flows.

Canada's economic experience, both in the past and more recently, provides lessons of interest to other countries that share the hemisphere with a dominant economic power also more technologically advanced. Canada's involvement in the same trading system substantially dilutes U.S. economic and political dominance. Of additional value to LAC in all these issues is Canada's long experience in close trade and investment relationships with the United States and the learning that has accompanied it.

Canadian Technical and Industrial Expertise and Direct Investment

Although not as diverse as the United States, the Canadian economy is highly productive in many sectors and has developed pockets of comparative advantage along with technical skills relevant to several of the countries of Latin America. In primary industries such as forest products, wheat and other agricultural products, and nickel, iron, and other minerals, current or recent Canadian technologies could be useful in LAC countries. For example, forest products could benefit Argentina, Brazil, Peru, and others; agricultural technology could be particularly useful for Argentina; and nickel production technology could assist the Colombian industry.

Of great relevance to Latin American countries is Canada's experience in the transition to high productivity, high-tech, and service industries, as well as the expertise Canada can now provide in a number of those areas. Particularly interesting is the experience of the province of Quebec, which has evolved from a primary product-oriented region to one that is now the base for some of Canada's front-rank firms and industries. This is the sort of achievement to which many countries of Latin America aspire, especially when considering that thirty years ago the province of Quebec had to confront both a relatively backward industrial sector and an underdeveloped educational system.

Canada as a Development Model

Like most countries in the LAC, Canada had its phase of primary product exports, followed by (though also overlapping with) a stage of import-substituting development in which it fostered domestic industry and encouraged "tariff factories" behind protectionist barriers. Additionally, Canada has felt the continuing tension between a fear of freer trade with and investment from the U.S. and a belief that its own productivity and competitiveness depend on freer trade and investment flows.

Like most of LAC, Canada's international economic relationships gradually shifted from an early focus on Europe to one on the United States, a natural response to geographical proximity, similar life-styles, and a capacity to get along with each other. The tight economic ties in a naturally asymmetric power relationship led Canadians to wonder (as many still do) whether economic dependency would gradually lead to greater and greater political and cultural dependency. In terms of economic size, Canada is about equal to Brazil and Mexico combined. It is 60 percent as large as Latin America and the Caribbean as a whole. Canada thus shares, both with individual countries like Mexico and Brazil and with the region as a whole, the experience of economic association with a dominant power at least eight times larger. Few countries in the world have had Canada's experience of such focused economic interaction over such a long period of time with a much larger partner. For this reason, there is much to be learned from Canada's economic history.

Though it has passed through phases of development similar to those characteristic of Latin America, Canada has always remained a relatively open economy. Because of its long-standing commitment to multilateralism and freer trade, Canada has progressively reduced barriers. Many studies exist on the impacts of reduced barriers, analyzing how trade and investment liberalization have affected the structure of industry and trade, labor markets and wages, and income and welfare. These could be of great value to the LAC countries.

As the only other high-income country in the Western Hemisphere besides the United States, Canada offers interesting alternatives to the U.S. model. It has been somewhat less inclined to the free market model or to the ideology of individualism, as reflected in its widely praised (though now financially vulnerable) socialized health care system and its more publicly funded educational system.

Like many LAC countries, Canada is regionally quite diverse, not only in topography but, more relevantly, in terms of cultural and economic characteristics. It has two main languages. It has regions based primarily on the production and export of primary products, others where import-substituting and export-oriented manufacturing activities are heavily concentrated, and still others that are considerably better off and more dynamic. The federal political system has meant that many regional conflicts and differences of preference have manifested themselves in negotiations and compromises involving both federal and provincial governments.

These elements are crucial in distinguishing Canada from the United States. Thus, while LAC countries would like greater access to U.S. markets, the Canadian development model provides a perspective on how two-way access can be achieved through freer trade and investment as well as how to maintain independent economic, cultural, and political values.

The 1989 GDP of Latin America was only 13.6 percent of the combined GDP of the United States plus Latin America. When Canada and Latin America are combined, their share of the Western Hemisphere GDP is a more substantial 20 percent. While the United States does a higher share of its trading outside the hemisphere, both LAC and Canada have trade patterns in which the United States features very prominently. Though this obviously creates an asymmetrical relationship, it also means that, in absolute terms, the flows in each direction are of comparable magnitudes. For example, in 1988 the essentially balanced U.S.-Latin America trade flows accounted for only 10 to 11 percent of U.S. trade, while Canada accounted for 21.6 percent of U.S. exports and 18.7 percent of its imports. Thus, the inclusion of Canada in a trading region greatly increases the importance of that region to the United States. Nevertheless, it is hard to predict the ways in which Canada's inclusion might affect negotiations and outcomes. The large absolute size of Canadian-U.S. trade clearly makes it relevant to question whether it would diminish the power of the United States in the bargaining process and avoid the Canadian LAC losses resulting from the imposition of the hub and spoke model.

Summary

G iven Canada's limited economic ties with Latin America, why should the EAI be of interest to Canadian citizens, business people, or politicians? The answer involves both simple, direct economic effects and more general, political-economic ones. The potential for significant economic gains is suggested by the current low level of such trade. That low level may signal potential but unrealized "gains from trade." Moreover, as Latin America grows and opens up, opportunities for Canadian exports and investment in that region will multiply. The other side of the coin is a potential economic cost to Canada resulting from increased competition for Canadian goods in U.S. and Canadian markets.

A second type of benefit is less immediate and has a political as well as an economic aspect. For Canada, a small nation with a population of 26 million people and heavily tied to the North American market, there are potential benefits from a spreading WHFTA which will develop institutions and rules-based mechanisms for preventing any country's use or abuse of unilateral powers. In fact, Canada's main agenda has always been to develop multilateral rules and institutions. This "small country agenda" would be advanced by the expansion of the CUSFTA into a larger, multilateral trading area. On the negative side, LAC countries may complicate the long-standing Canada-U.S. relationship by adding new elements and obscuring the decades of progress.

Other questions of costs and benefits deal with the impact of an EAI on the changes now taking place in the "architecture" of North America's economic, political, legal, and corporate systems. To what extent, for example, will Canadian interests in LAC be reshaped or intensified as a result of the process of regional change described above? Is it likely that a common "North American" perspective on LAC will evolve? If that is the case, what is the impact on Mexico? How will political and economic patterns be affected, since it is more likely that particular regions in Canada and the United States will develop more intensive interests in LAC than others?

Four reasons come to mind when looking from South to North and determining why Latin America should care whether or not Canada is involved.

First, Canada has expertise in a number of areas, related in part to its successful experiences while developing within a relatively inhospitable climate. This is reflected by Canada's comparative advantage in various product lines that could be available to LAC by means of direct investment or other types of technological transfer. Second, Canada is home to many multinationals and is the world's fourth largest capital exporter on a per capita basis. Third, Canada provides a development model of interest to LAC that includes phases of capital imports, import-substitution, and trade liberalization. As recently as the first decade of this century, Uruguay and Argentina had per capita incomes comparable to Canada's, although they have since fallen far behind. Why did this happen? Fourth, Canada has a long history of trade, investment, and political ties with the United States. This experience is of great relevance to countries in the Western Hemisphere contemplating closer ties.

Canada has concentrated its economic ties on the United States. Yet, as the countries of Latin America and the Caribbean open to trade and investment in a series of pacts, the opportunity exists for Canada to gaze beyond the Rio Grande. Canadian hesitation with EAI rests on its concentration on the U.S. market, the fear that its preferences in U.S. markets will erode, and the threat of Canadian industry suffering from more direct competition. However, all Canadians realize that to be stranded at the northern tip of the hemisphere, outside a large trade and investment pact, is a risky long-term strategy. Thus, EAI forces Canada's policy to be one of "reluctant regionalism." While important economic and political gains can be gained from EAI, these gains will require Canadian politicians, and primarily Canadian business people, aggressively to pursue LAC markets and other ties.

Notes

[1] In 1989, the stock of Canadian investment in the United Kingdom exceeded Canadian-held investment in LAC. Canadian investment in LAC, however, exceeds Canadian investment in Europe outside the UK.

[2] The following pages draw on a paper by Albert Berry, Leonard Waverman, and Ann Weston, 1992, "Canada and the Enterprise for the Americas Initiative: A Case of Reluctant Regionalism," *Business Economics* (April), which itself drew on a paper by Ann Weston called "Trade Bargaining in Canada and the U.S.: Drifting Towards Regionalism?" with funding from the International Development Research Center.

[3] For example, the Economic Council of Canada (1988) concluded that sectoral policies had retarded rather than promoted adjustment to change. It recommended that general labor adjustment policies — for example, the expansion of the Industrial Adjustment Service — be substituted for capital subsidies.

[4] As in the United States, it is important in the Canadian case to distinguish between federal and sub-federal policies. The Quebec provincial government, in particular, has continued to adopt an interventionist industrial policy in various high-tech and other sectors (for example, aluminum processing and power projects). The Ontario government has also initiated a more active industrial policy, and there are several other examples of provincial support. How far these are compatible with the obligations of the CUSFTA remains to be seen.

[5] EAI, announced by former President George Bush in June 1990, calls for hemispheric trade integration, investment assistance ($1.5 billion), and debt reduction for Latin American and Caribbean countries.

[6] Additionally, if it turns out that trade liberalization leads to much better growth performance in the LAC region, Canada would share the benefits from this "indirect" effect. The evidence is not yet in on this question. Chile is the only LAC country to have liberalized long enough ago to provide any test, and its subsequent performance has shown signs of attaining strong sustained growth. Mexico's liberalization is too recent to assess in any meaningful way.

[7] Canadian firms, such as Northern Telecom, do have substantial business in Mexico; these sales likely appear as U.S. exports since they come from U.S. plants.

[8] This is a variant of a proposition by Stigler (1971) who argues that regulation of private activities (such as medicine or architecture) increases the power of the smaller members.

[9] See, for example, Eric Hobsbawn (1987), chapters 2-6. See also Sidney Pollard (1981), especially chapter 7. In addition, a very neat, brief description

of the economic and social context of the mass production system is found in James P. Womack, Daniel T. Jones, and Daniel Roos (1990), chapter 2.

[10] Allan E. Gotlieb, speech at the Americas Society, New York, on November 25, 1991.

[11] Canadian investment in LAC is greater than Canadian investment in Europe outside the EC.

[12] This section is based on Berry, Waverman, and Weston (1992).

References

Berry, Albert, Leonard Waverman, and Ann Weston. 1992. "Canada and the Enterprise for the Americas Initiative: A Case of Reluctant Regionalism." *Business Economics* (April).

Hobsbawn, Eric. 1987. *The Age of Empire 1875 - 1914.* New York: Pantheon Books.

Krugman, Paul, ed. 1986. *Strategic Trade Policy and the New International Economics.* Cambridge, Mass.: M.I.T. Press.

Lipsey, Richard. 1990. "Canada and the U.S.-Mexico Free Trade Dance: Wallflower or Partner." *Commentary #20* (August).

Markusen, J., and R. Wigle. 1990. "Explaining the Volume of North-South Trade." *Economic Journal* 100 (December).

New York Times, July 22, 1990.

Ohmae, Kenichi. 1990. *The Borderless World.* New York: Doubleday.

Ohmae, Kenichi. 1990a. "Toward a Global Regionalization." *Wall Street Journal.* April 27.

Pollard, Sidney. 1981. *Peaceful Conquest: The Industrialization of Europe 1760 - 1970.* Oxford: Oxford University Press.

Porter, Michael. 1990. *The Competitive Advantage of Nations.* New York: The Free Press.

Porter, Michael. 1990a. "Japan Isn't Playing by Different Rules." *New York Times,* July 22.

Porter, Michael. 1990b. *Harvard Business Review* (March/April).

Schrage, Michael. 1990. "Should California Be G-8?" *International Economy* (October/December).

Sigler, John. 1971. "A Theory of Regulation." *Bell Journal of Economics and Management Science.* (Autumn).

Wallace, William. 1990. *The Transformation of Western Europe.* New York: Council on Foreign Relations.

Womack, James, Daniel Roos, and Daniel T. Jones. 1990. *The Machine that Changed the World.* New York: Macmillan.

Wonnacott, Ronald. 1990. *U.S. Hub-and-Spoke Bilateral and the Multilateral Trading System: C.D. Howe Institute Commentary 23.* Toronto: C.D. Howe Institute (October).

Chapter II

CANADA AND LATIN AMERICA: THE EVOLUTION OF INSTITUTIONAL TIES

Stephen J. Randall

The decision by the Conservative government of Brian Mulroney in late 1989 to seek membership in the Organization of American States (OAS) ended decades of speculation, debate, uncertainty, and ambiguity about the formal Canadian role in Latin America. Those decades of uncertainty over the formal relationship of Canada to the Pan-American Union (PAU) and OAS, however, masked a substantial degree of political and economic involvement by Canada in Latin American affairs.

This paper outlines the main features of that political and economic involvement since the early twentieth century with specific attention to the development of bilateral and multilateral institutional ties. The first part focuses on the political and organizational history of that involvement, including developments since Canada joined the OAS. The second part discusses the economic dimensions of Canadian involvement, treating such issues as trade agreements, cooperation in the area of communications, and other technical matters. It examines trade promotion agencies such as the Export Development Corporation (EDC), assesses the specific role of Canadian foreign aid (particularly the Canadian International Development Agency — CIDA), and reviews Canada's participation in the Inter-American Development Bank (IDB) and within the United Nations (UN).[1]

Stephen J. Randall is Chair in American Studies, Faculty of Social Sciences, at The University of Calgary.

I would like to thank Mr. Peter Zyla, a graduate student in political science at the University of Calgary, for his conscientious research work in the preparation of this article. (S.J.R.)

Canada and the Inter-American System

In the early 1820s, when Simón Bolívar first conceived the idea of a Pan-American system based on mutual interests against Europe, Canada was still an embryo within the womb of the British Empire — the remainder of the hemisphere, except Puerto Rico, Cuba, the Guianas, and parts of the West Indies, had already broken the umbilical cord with European imperialism. That continued legacy of Canada as part of the British Empire and later the Commonwealth was a major factor in shaping the extent to which Canada was either inclined or able to play a role in the evolving inter-American system. Anti-European sentiment, which was particularly pronounced in the United States and embodied in the Monroe Doctrine, placed Canada in an awkward position with respect to its aspirations for a higher level of involvement in the inter-American system.

As a British colony without formal autonomous recognition until the 1931 Statute of Westminster and without its own constitution until the 1980s, until World War II Canada seemed more a reminder of the old world order in the hemisphere than a participant in the new. Moreover, Canada was not only a remnant of British imperialism but also increasingly a branch plant economy for the United States from the late nineteenth century onward. This was hardly a feature that would endear it to Latin America.

After U.S. Secretary of State James G. Blaine revived the inter-American system in the 1880s, contributing to the establishment of the Commercial Bureau of the American Republics and the PAU, there was considerable expectation that Canada ultimately would find its way into the organization. Nonetheless, the U.S. congressional resolution approving the holding of the 1889 Pan American Conference did not include Canada despite preliminary consideration of inviting Canada (Mecham 1961).

The reasons for Canada's aloofness from the PAU and, subsequently, the OAS were complex and often emotional. They ranged from Canada's lack of real independence from Britain before World War II to its traditional economic, political, cultural, and strategic ties to Europe, and by World War II to a degree of U.S. hostility toward an expanded Canadian role in the inter-American system.[2] Furthermore, from the perspective of many Canadian governments, the OAS, ever since its founding in Bogotá in 1948, was designed as an instrument of U.S. Cold War policy. The Rio Treaty of Mutual Defense was an integral part — indeed, the crown jewel — in the OAS edifice, and Canadians did not like to be drawn too deeply into U.S. Cold War policies. Canadian Liberal Prime Minister William Lyon MacKenzie King viewed Latin America and the Spanish Caribbean as being solidly within the U.S. sphere of influence, and he was reluctant to become embroiled in the region if it meant potential friction with the United States (Rochlin 1991). Instead, Canada became a charter member of the North Atlantic Treaty Organization (NATO), fulfilling its commitment of containing Soviet communism in Europe and cooperating fully with the United States in establishing an increasingly integrated North American defense establishment which was embodied in the North American Aerospace Defense Command (NORAD) during the 1950s.

The World War II years, nonetheless, witnessed considerable expansion in formal Canadian ties with Latin America. By 1946 Canada had established independent diplomatic relations with Brazil, Argentina, Chile, Cuba, Venezuela, Mexico, and Peru, partly reflecting the economic importance of those countries to Canadian interests (King 1944, 5912). Significantly, Canada inaugurated diplomatic relations with Argentina and Chile in 1941 at a time when Canada was at war with Germany and both Argentine and Chilean officials were inclined toward Nazi and fascist sympathies. Cold War diversions — preoccupation with the United States and Europe, Latin American instability, and the realities of Canadian trade patterns — all conspired in the 1950s to keep Canadian official involvement in Latin America to a minimum. As Minister of Trade and Commerce, C. D. Howe led a much-publicized commercial mission to Latin America in 1953. However, little of consequence emerged from it. In general, the prime ministers during the 1940s through early 1960s, including Louis Saint Laurent, John Diefenbaker, and former Secretary of State for Foreign Affairs Lester Pearson, tended to be Europhiles. Especially in the case of Pearson, Canadian leaders were highly conscious of the U.S. economic and political link and were loathe to risk alienating Canadian allies for the sake of a tenuous expansion into a Latin America that remained terra incognita for most Canadians.

Although formally outside the OAS, Canada quietly participated in inter-American organizations under OAS auspices during this period. During the 1960s and 1970s, Canadian activity in the region increased, although there was a tendency for activity to focus on the

Commonwealth Caribbean. By 1966 Canada was a member of the Commonwealth Caribbean-Canada Trade and Economic Committee, and by 1971 it had joined the Caribbean Development Bank, the Centre for Latin American Monetary Studies, and the Pan American Health Organization. It had also established a Canada-Mexico Joint Committee and joined the Inter-American Centre of Tax Administrators.

Canada either participated directly or sent observers to a wide range of inter-American conferences and meetings of varying significance in the post-World War II years. These conferences ran the spectrum from technical and statistical sessions, to sessions on health, social security, migration, tourism, education, labor and trade unions, industrial development, transportation, and criminology. Striking in their absence were conferences relating to national security and defense matters, a clear indication of the issues that Canadian officials wished to avoid. Altogether, Canadian officials participated either as direct delegates or as observers at more than one hundred twenty official inter-American conferences from 1949 to 1971. Canada was granted official OAS permanent observer status in 1972.

At first glance, it might appear ironic that it was Anglophile John Diefenbaker who pressed most vigorously in the late 1950s and early 1960s for an expansion of Canadian involvement in the Western Hemisphere. His first Secretary of State for External Affairs, Sidney Smith, and Smith's successor, Howard Green, displayed more interest in Latin America than their predecessors. As a result, in late 1958 Canada sent another trade mission to Brazil, Peru, and Mexico. Of seminal symbolic importance, External Affairs established a Latin American Division in 1960. By the end of 1961, Canada had established diplomatic relations with all the independent nations in the region and, again with considerable significance, did not follow the lead of the United States and the OAS in breaking diplomatic relations with or establishing economic sanctions against Fidel Castro's Cuba.

Canada's Cuban policy was not based on pure altruism, nor was it premised primarily on anti-American assumptions or strong differences of view with the United States over the Cold War. There was a Canadian tendency to view Latin American revolutionary movements more as the product of indigenous groups and dislocation rather than as Soviet imports. Canada logically followed the British lead and that of other European powers in maintaining its Cuban links. Cuba offered Canadian business interests potential markets for goods and investment as well as a source of sugar and tropical products not available in Canada.

The Canadian view of the Cold War in Cuba was not as distinct from that of the United States as might appear by its maintaining diplomatic and commercial ties. Certainly, there were strains between the Kennedy administration and the Conservative government of John Diefenbaker as John F. Kennedy brought pressure on the Canadian government to toe the line on Cuba and its Soviet links, particularly during the 1962 Missile Crisis. Yet, on another level the Canadian presence in Cuba was convenient for the United States, providing a window of opportunity to view internal Cuban events, and Canada obliged by furnishing information to the Central Intelligence Agency (CIA) (Jackson 1983).

The Diefenbaker government's apparent expansion of interest in Latin American ties sparked renewed speculation and debate about Canadian membership in the OAS. However, that debate was short-lived and tended to echo old arguments about U.S. dominance in the organization and the priority of traditional Canadian orientation toward the Commonwealth, NATO, North American defense, and the Commonwealth Caribbean. Kennedy administration pressures on the Diefenbaker government to raise its hemispheric commitment to the Cold War undercut any further likelihood of a Canadian move toward the OAS for the remainder of the decade. The election of Lester Pearson as Liberal Prime Minister simply consolidated that orientation. Pearson's Secretary of State for External Affairs, Paul Martin, stood alone within government circles as an enthusiastic advocate for Canadian membership in the OAS and an expanded Canadian role in hemisphere affairs (Ogelsby 1979).

By the time the Liberal government of Pierre Elliott Trudeau conducted a thorough review of Canadian foreign policy, bilateral and multilateral linkages with Latin America were extensive. For instance, in addition to some of the programs enumerated above, there were cooperative programs in science and technology. Pierre Elliott Trudeau's search for a Third Option in foreign policy after 1968 left no place for a U.S. Cold War instrument such as the OAS. This matter remained quiescent until the departure of Trudeau and the election of the Conservative Party under Brian Mulroney in 1984.

Nonetheless, the Trudeau government's thorough but often controversial search for new directions in Canadian foreign policy did have implications for Canada-Latin America linkages. Trudeau and some of his close associates were personally and intellectually more interested in Latin America than any of their predecessors. This fact can be explained, in part, by the greater degree of cultural, intellectual, and linguistic affinity for Latin America that had long existed among French Canadians as compared to English Canadians. Additionally, the fact that Trudeau's search for a Third Option would inevitably draw Canadian policy into closer harmony with the Third World (and perhaps into conflict with prevailing U.S. assumptions about the Cold War in the Western Hemisphere) also helps explain the French Canadian interest.

One should not exaggerate this interest in Latin America, however, as an affinity with Latin American political and economic radicalism. French Canadian Roman Catholicism displayed the same strand of strong anti-communism that was evident among Roman Catholics in the United States and elsewhere, but neither Trudeau nor his contemporary French Canadian intellectuals were inclined to share the parochial views of the Roman Catholic Church hierarchy. Furthermore, Trudeau brought into the cabinet individuals of like mind with personal interests in Latin America, including his long-time associate Gerard Pelletier. Pelletier had traveled extensively in Latin America as Paul Martin's parliamentary secretary, and he called for an expanded Canadian economic, cultural, and development role in Latin America (Ogelsby 1979).

The Trudeau reassessment of Canadian foreign policy under Secretary of State for External Affairs Mitchell Sharp inevitably touched on Latin America. As part of the process, the Liberal government sent a major mission to nine Latin American countries in the fall of 1968. The mission's report became part of the broader review of Canadian foreign policy which was embodied in the Canadian Department of External Affairs (DEA) 1970 publications: *Foreign Policy for Canadians* and *Foreign Policy for Canadians: Latin America.*

The latter publication touched on the critical and traditional areas of Canadian-Latin American relations: natural environment, social justice, economic growth, peace and security, development assistance, multilateral institutions, trade, investment, migration and immigration, and the perennial issue of OAS membership. The main arguments and assumptions of that twenty-year-old report on Canada and Latin America continue to be applied in the 1990s. It suggested that Latin

America's role in the world would continue to grow, that the historical U.S. role — geographically and in policy terms — had tended to screen Latin America from Canada, and that Canadians had gradually become more sensitive to the fact that their nation was "firmly rooted in the Western Hemisphere" with a role to play in the region (DEA 1970a). The U.S. position in the hemisphere would continue to condition the role of Canada.

The report suggested that U.S. hegemony "will cast Canada in the role of a middle power in the hemisphere, and it will pose a challenge to Canadians to maintain their own cultural and entrepreneurial identity when dealing with Latin Americans" (DEA 1970a, 5-6). At the same time, the imbalance of power between Canada and the United States should not mask the existence of common economic interests nor the fact that Latin Americans tend to look to Canada as a possible counterweight against U.S. hegemony. The report also observed Canada's rather exceptional place in the Commonwealth Caribbean despite traditional American predominance in what had been considered an "American lake since the turn of the century." The DEA concluded that an expansion of ties with Latin America would, in fact, "strengthen Canadian sovereignty and independence," "enrich" Canadian cultural life, and expand the Canadian role in international affairs (DEA 1970a, 6-7).

Foreign Policy for Canadians: Latin America carefully reviewed the debate over Canadian membership in the OAS. It observed that the OAS had acquired a greater degree of "dynamism" in planning and administration and that the composition of the organization had undergone an evolution with the acceptance of three Commonwealth Caribbean nations: Barbados, Jamaica, and Trinidad and Tobago. The DEA review portrayed the OAS as a logical forum within which economic and social questions as well as political and security problems might be debated and resolved. The critical issue from the perspective of Canadian officials was the extent to which the OAS could evolve into an organization that dealt effectively with economic and social issues and become less of a regional collective security organization under U.S. control.

For the moment, however, there was concern that membership in the organization would hamper the flexibility of Canadian "freedom of action" regarding development assistance. There was an additional general problem for Canada with respect to financial costs of membership and the need to work through such bodies as the Inter-American Council for Education, Science, and Culture, which could potentially assign a lower priority to the development of any bilateral cultural programs. In short, the report concluded that any decision to seek membership in the OAS would be based upon the recognition that there existed a certain regionalization trend in the world. The DEA did not recommend a direct quest for membership at that time but rather an effort to build additional links with individual Latin American countries and selected multilateral institutions, "thus preparing for whatever role it may in future be called upon to play in the Western Hemisphere" (DEA 1970a, 20-24).

For the next fifteen years, *Foreign Policy for Canadians: Latin America* remained the formal basis for policy initiatives. The most dramatic development in policy, however, came in late 1989 with the decision of the Conservative government of Brian Mulroney to seek Canadian membership in the OAS. Although that decision may have appeared to be a radical departure from previous policy and official attitudes, there was considerable foreshadowing of it in *Foreign Policy for Canadians.* There also existed a substantial foundation of Canadian involvement in bilateral and multilateral organizations that made the Canadian entry into the OAS both smooth and predictable.

By the late 1980s, Canada was very active as a permanent member of the Pan-American Health Organization, the Inter-American Institute for Cooperation in Agriculture, and the Pan-American Institute for Geography and History. In 1987 Canada hosted the Ninth Inter-American Conference of Ministers of Agriculture and the Fourth Regular Meeting of the Inter-American Board of Agriculture in Ottawa. Prior to the decision to join the OAS, the position of ambassador was relocated to Ottawa, although the Permanent Observer Mission to the OAS remained in Washington. In addition, the new position of roving ambassador was created, and there was a stated effort to strengthen Latin American ties and to emphasize to the Canadian public the growing importance of the region in Canadian policy (DEA 1987). Ironically, however, the decision came at a time when the OAS and the inter-American system, in general, seemed to have failed in meeting a basic precondition identified in 1970 — the primacy of economic and social development over military and national security issues. In 1989 Nicaragua and El Salvador were still in the throes of bloody and prolonged decade-old civil wars in which the United States and Cuba were major players and in which anachronistic Cold War assumptions about social and economic revolution appeared to be driving the policies of both the Reagan and Bush administrations in Washington.

Canadian Secretary of State for External Affairs Joe Clark informed a Calgary audience in February 1990 that the Canadian decision to join the OAS was a reflection of the larger trajectory of Canadian foreign policy — to pursue a distinctive Canadian role in international relations involving steady pressure and tangible support for peaceful change. Clark placed the Canadian position on Latin America within a framework which included South African policy and involvement in efforts to bring peace to Cambodia. To Clark, Canada had major interests and real influence in Latin America because, as he claimed, "Many of the problems which plague the globe have a direct relation to Latin America." He vigorously rejected the contention that Canadian membership in the OAS would either lead to U.S. dominance of the Canadian position within the OAS or to conflicts with the United States that might compromise the Canadian position on issues it viewed as important. Clark conceded that one of the persistent problems within the OAS was the tendency of Latin American and U.S. agendas to polarize, but he suggested that Latin American members believed that Canada might serve to mitigate that polarization (DEA 1990).

The debate over Canadian membership in the OAS took place within the context of the December 1989 U.S. invasion of Panama. The Canadian government expressed regret at the American action, criticizing the use of force as a dangerous precedent and noting that the OAS charter condemns the principle of intervention in the internal affairs of member states. It also expressed understanding of the circumstances that had led to the U.S. action.

The larger diplomatic context was the continued quest for negotiated peace in Central America. In the course of the 1980s, the five Central American governments had sought Canadian involvement through the United Nations in helping to design a peacekeeping mission. In late 1989 the UN Security Council adopted a resolution creating a security verification group to supervise an eventual peace in Central America. In accordance with that resolution, Canada provided approximately one hundred unarmed military personnel to participate in the United Nations Observers for Central America (ONUCA) to monitor the demobilization of the contras in Nicaragua and a cease-fire in El Salvador, which concludes with an agreement between the Christiani government in El Salvador and the Faribundo Martí Liberation Front.

Canada, in particular through Elections Canada, also played an important role in the February 1990 Nicaraguan national elections that resulted in the defeat of the FSLN government of Daniel Ortega and the election of Violeta Chamorro. In addition to the provision of technical, material, and advisory support to the Supreme Electoral Council of Nicaragua, Canada provided a team of election monitors attached to both the UN observation group (ONUVEN) and to the OAS observation team. The following year Canada played a similar though reduced role through the OAS in the El Salvador congressional elections. The United Nations did not participate.[3] In 1991 the Canadian government also sent election observers to Suriname. The Canadian government has since cooperated with the OAS in an effort to resolve the political crisis in Haiti associated with the military overthrow of its constitutionally elected government. Clearly, on the public stage the Canadian transformation from observer status to formal OAS membership has been a comparatively smooth one.

Economic Linkages

This section is concerned with the institutional economic linkages between Canada and Latin America rather than with general patterns of trade and private foreign investment. Hence, Canada's place in such agencies as the Caribbean Development Bank, the IDB, and the United Nations Economic Commission for Latin America and the Caribbean (ECLAC) is examined. This is not to downplay the importance of private foreign investment and trade but rather to focus attention on formal Canadian government links. Indeed, for many years, Latin America has been second only to the United States as a target for Canadian foreign investment. It is well-known that Canadian banks have been active in the region since early in the twentieth century; in fact, the Royal Bank of Canada established its first operations in Latin America at about the same time that it established its first branch in Ontario.

By the mid-1970s, Canadian foreign investment in Latin America had reached $2.3 billion, the bulk of which was in Brazil (Gignac 1979). In terms of Canadian-Latin American trade, in 1987 Canada exported over $1.5 billion in goods to Mexico, the Caribbean, and Central

America and imported slightly more than $2 billion. The majority of that trade was with Cuba, Mexico, and Puerto Rico. With respect to South America, Canada exported more than $5 billion in goods and imported more than $1.4 billion; the overwhelming majority of this trade was with Brazil, Venezuela, Colombia, and Peru. This is reflective of the importance of oil and other extractive industry ties (DEA 1987, 59-60). Canadian agencies that have been most active in establishing economic development linkages with Latin America have been the Export Development Corporation (EDC) and the Canadian International Development Agency (CIDA), although the International Development Research Council (IDRC) and a variety of NGOs have also played a part in the process.

Since the 1960s Canadian governments, both Conservative and Liberal, have seen an important role for Canadian trade, loans, and development assistance in Latin America. The government has viewed trade and industrial development, investment, and export financing as the means of international cooperation. One of the main areas of Canadian contribution to Latin America and the Caribbean by the late 1970s was in the area of technology transfer. During the 1980s Petro-Canada International Assistance Corporation (PCIAC) developed imaginative and constructive programs in which Canadian engineers, geologists, chemists, and other technical experts worked with Latin American state oil enterprises, such as ECOPETROL in Colombia and YPFB in Bolivia, in order to improve research and development in the oil and natural gas sectors.[4]

The oil industry is only one area in which the Canadian government and its agencies have played a significant role. Through various agencies — in particular, CIDA and the IDB — Canada has been involved in other areas in the development of dry-farming techniques, improved forestry, fishery, mineral prospecting techniques, railway planning and building, remote sensing, earthquake detection, hydro-electric power grids, heavy oil technology, nuclear energy, and distance education. Canadian officials have observed that such technology and information transfer has not been only one-directional. For instance, Canadians have learned topographical and thematic mapping techniques which are useful in the Arctic areas from Brazilian, Colombian, and Mexican specialists. Canadian scientists have also made use of Brazilian research in the field of earth physics — notably, geodesy, gravity, and geodynamics.[5]

Although small in comparison to that of the United States and more recently Japan, Canada's financial participation in the IDB has been significant. Although Canada had been active in Bank projects for almost a decade, it officially joined the IDB in May 1972. IDB membership was essential if Canada was to play a role in hemispheric economic development. The decision to join the IDB coincided with the establishment of Canada's permanent observer status at the OAS. Both decisions stemmed logically from the Trudeau review of Canadian foreign policy. Significantly, Canada was the only new member of the IDB during the 1970s that contributed but did not borrow from the Bank, even though in the early 1970s the Canadian contribution was one-third that of Brazil and one-half that of Mexico (Gignac 1979).

There were also economic advantages to Canadian involvement in the IDB. Prior to formal membership, Canadian suppliers were eligible only to bid on projects funded from the IDB's ordinary capital. As a full member, Canada also became eligible to supply goods and services for projects financed by IDB loans from the Fund for Special Operations and from the C$1.5 million Canadian Project Preparation Fund established in 1974. The objective of the Canadian Project Preparation Fund was to finance the preparation of Latin American development projects to include basic studies, feasibility studies, and final engineering design studies. Not surprisingly, this initiative prompted several hundred Canadian firms to register as consultants with the IDB.

Canada's initial contribution to the IDB involved subscription to more than $642 million of the IDB's ordinary capital resources and $60 million to the Fund for Special Operations (Gignac 1979). By the end of 1977, Canada had contributed approximately $700 million to IDB projects. In addition, Canada contributed $127 million to the IDB Fund for Special Operations which enables the Bank to provide financial resources on a long-term, low-interest rate basis for social development projects. By use of complementary financing, between 1972 and 1977, the IDB channeled approximately $145 million into Latin America through private banks, including three Canadian private banks — Bank of Nova Scotia, the Royal Bank of Canada, and the Banque Canadienne Nationale.

Although the IDB continues to sponsor social and educational development programs, during the 1980s it seemed to shift increasingly toward encouraging private sector investment, perhaps in keeping with the spirit and letter of the Reagan administration's Caribbean Basin

Initiative (CBI) and the Bush administration's EAI. In 1991 the IDB approved a record high $5.4 billion in loans. For the first time, in 1971 the IDB approved funds for Latin American foreign debt reduction and investment sector reform. In a measure that grew directly out of EAI, in February 1992 the IDB, the United States, and twenty-one other "American" countries including Canada signed an agreement creating a Multilateral Investment Fund (MIF) of more than $1.5 billion. The main objectives of the MIF program are to reduce the region's external debt, encourage a significant increase in private foreign investment in the area, promote privatization and trade liberalization, enhance the basic skills of smaller business enterprises, and support the restructuring of work forces. Its underlying philosophy is to "build economic systems where the private sector is the engine of future growth" (IDB 1992, 8-9). The Canadian contribution to the International Monetary Fund (IMF) is reported at $30.7 million, equal to each of the contributions by Germany, Italy, and Spain. It is the largest contribution from the Western Hemisphere after the $500 million pledge from the United States, but it is dwarfed by Japan's.

CIDA's main contributions have been in forestry, agriculture, fisheries, and hydro-electricity. Although CIDA's level of funding tends not to be as significant as that from the IDB, Canadian involvement in development outside the IDB has been substantial.

In addition to those two main channels of assistance, the Canadian government has played a role in other multilateral bodies, such as the World Bank, and in subregional organizations, such as the Andean Pact in which Canada has been interested since its formation in the 1960s. Other multilateral forums for Latin American development to which Canada contributes include the United Nations Commission on Trade and Development (UNCTAD), the IMF, GATT, and ECLAC, where Canada was especially active in the late 1970s in its support of the Latin American Demographic Center.

The EDC has been the main agent for the financing of Canadian exports to Latin America. From 1961 to 1976, the EDC signed export financing agreements involving insured export credits with most Latin American countries which facilitated Canadian trade with those nations. Brazil, Mexico, and Venezuela were the main recipients, although Jamaica also figured prominently.

Exports financed included the supply of equipment, technical assistance, and project management services for airport modernization in Cuba; electric transmission equipment, chlorine dioxide plant and related equipment and services, and equipment and services for an offshore oil production system for Brazil; equipment and services for nickel mining and processing facilities in Guatemala; and equipment and services for the rehabilitation and expansion of the national railway system in Peru (EDC 1976).

Nonetheless, when compared with other areas of the world, the Caribbean and Latin America have not been the highest priority in EDC activities. In 1985, for instance, Mexico and Central America represented only 4 percent of EDC export financing and South America only 15 percent, in comparison with 28 percent for Western Europe and 15 percent for North and West Africa.[6] It is debatable how important the EDC's work is in promoting trade activity with Latin America. Nevertheless, a good deal of Canadian export trade with Latin America in non-traditional sectors probably would not take place without the EDC's contribution. When data is presented in terms of global Canadian foreign assistance (from CIDA, IDRC, the Department of Finance, PCIAC, and the International Centre for Ocean Development), the level of financial support during the 1980s was substantial: $2.5 billion in 1986-87 (CIDA 1986-87).

By the late 1980s, another area of Canadian institutional involvement in the Caribbean and Latin America began with the attempt to control narcotics trafficking. To that end Canada participated in the Barbados Drug Enforcement Conference in March 1988, which involved Latin American countries, Britain, and the United States (DEA 1987). Canada has also provided technical assistance in recent years to assist Colombian police and drug enforcement authorities in their efforts to bring narcotics traffic under control.

These areas are suggestive of the nature and the extent of recent Canadian political and economic linkages with Latin America. The economic recession, the emergence of serious negotiations over NAFTA and other possible hemispheric linkages, and the implications of EAI may serve to strengthen those ties.

Notes

[1] NGOs and military relations are treated in other chapters of this volume.

[2] J.C.M. Ogelsby, 1976, "Canada and Latin America," in Peyton Lyon and Tareq Ismael (eds.), *Canada and the Third World* (Toronto: MacMillan), 167. He more fully explores these early years in J.C.M. Oglesby, 1976, *Gringos from the Far North* (Toronto: MacMillan).

[3] This author participated as a UN observer in Nicaragua in 1990 and as a member of the OAS observation group in El Salvador in 1991.

[4] This author has served as a resource person in preparing PCIAC contract employees for their roles in working with Colombian and Bolivian development.

[5] See, for instance, the analysis of Canadian work in these fields by Jacques Gignac, 1979.

[6] Export Development Corporation, 1985, *Annual Report* (Ottawa: Queen's Printers), 13. The United States is classified with the Caribbean, thus making a Caribbean comparison impossible from EDC data.

References

Canadian International Development Agency. 1986-87. *Annual Report.* Ottawa: Queen's Printers.

Department of External Affairs, Canada. 1970. *Foreign Policy for Canadians.* Ottawa: Queen's Printers.

Department of External Affairs, Canada. 1970a. *Foreign Policy for Canadians: Latin America.* Ottawa: Queen's Printers.

Department of External Affairs, Canada. 1990. *Statements and Speeches: Notes for a Speech by the Right Honourable Joe Clark, Secretary of State for External Affairs, University of Calgary, On Canadian Policy Towards Latin America.* Presented in Calgary, Alberta on February 1.

Department of External Affairs, Canada. 1987. *Annual Report.* Ottawa: Queen's Printers.

Export Development Corporation. 1976. *Annual Report.* Ottawa: Queen's Printers.

Export Development Corporation. 1985. *Annual Report.* Ottawa: Queen's Printers.

Gignac, Jacques, Assistant Undersecretary of State for External Affairs, Information Services Division, DEA. 1979. Speech at the Plenary Meeting of the Forum das Americas. São Paulo, Brazil. June 12.

Inter-American Development Bank. 1974. *Canada and the Inter-American Development Bank.* Washington, D.C.: Inter-American Development Bank.

Inter-American Development Bank. 1972. *Report* (April). Washington, D.C.: Inter-American Development Bank.

Jackson, Robert. 1983. "Canadian Foreign Policy and the Western Hemisphere." *Governance in the Western Hemisphere.* New York: Praeger.

King, William Lyon MacKenzie. 1944. *Debates.* Statement to the House of Commons. Ottawa: Queen's Printers. August 4.

Mecham, J. Lloyd. 1961. *The United States and Inter-American Security, 1889-1960.* Austin, Texas: University of Texas Press.

Ogelsby, J.C.M. 1979. "A Trudeau Decade: Canadian-Latin American Relations, 1968-1978." *Journal of Interamerican Studies and World Affairs* 21:2 (May).

Ogelsby, J.C.M. 1976. "Canada and Latin America." In *Canada and the Third World,* eds. Peyton Lyon and Tareq Ismael. Toronto: MacMillan.

Ogelsby, J.C.M. 1976a. *Gringos from the Far North.* Toronto: MacMillan.

Randall, Stephen J. 1977. "Canada and the Development of Latin America." In *Foremost Nation: Canadian Foreign Policy and a Changing World,* eds. Norman Hillmer and Gartha Stevenson. Toronto: Gage.

Rochlin, James. 1991. "Canada, the Pan American Union and the Organization of American States." In *Canada and Latin America: Issues to the Year 2000,* eds. Stephen J. Randall and Mark O. Dickerson. Calgary: International Centre.

Chapter III

CANADA AND MIGRATION IN THE WESTERN HEMISPHERE

Alan B. Simmons

Before 1963 Canadian immigration policy virtually excluded LAC immigrants. Since that date, however, changes in Canadian immigration policy and a combination of political and economic conditions in the Caribbean and Latin America have led to a very rapid rise in migration from these regions to Canada. There are now sizable communities of LAC migrants in cities such as Toronto, Montreal, and Vancouver. They have established churches, newspapers, sports clubs, and neighborhoods which maintain cultural traditions and provide a supportive environment for new immigrants from the same regions. This chapter interprets these trends in terms of their relationship to the hemispheric political-economic system, Canadian immigration policies, and shifting international economic and cultural forces.

Rising migrant flows from the Caribbean and Latin America to Canada both reflect and contribute to Canada's expanding cultural and political linkages in the hemisphere. Two features of the emerging connection stand out. One is that migrant flows from these regions to Canada began recently — only twenty-five years ago. The other is that the migration linkage is largely restricted to two groups of countries: English-speaking nations in the Caribbean suffering from prolonged development crises and refugee-producing countries in Latin America.

This paper describes in greater detail the dominant trends in hemispheric migration affecting Canada. It also provides an interpretation of how these trends have been shaped by the Western Hemispheric "system" and by specific state policies and cultural linkages arising out of this system. Finally, it provides comments about future implications of current trends.

Alan B. Simmons is with the Centre for Research on Latin America and the Caribbean, York University.

Trends

Policy Evolution

National development in Canada throughout its entire history has been closely linked to programs favoring selective immigration and settlement (Hawkins 1991; Knowles 1992). At various times in the past, immigration policy has included the settlement of refugees, particularly in instances where they had skills as farmers or as workers in other important economic sectors (Basok and Simmons 1993; Dirks 1977). In this context, recent migration from LAC (and from other Third World regions) to Canada may be viewed as both a continuation of Canada's historically established pro-immigration policy and as a key illustration of how Canadian policies shifted in the 1960s. Canadian policy changed from a narrow, exclusionary focus (limiting immigration largely to Europeans) to one giving priority to the individual characteristics of immigrants rather than their country of origin or their racial or ethnic background.[1]

Throughout its entire history until the early 1960s, Canadian immigration policy virtually excluded migrants from places other than Europe. When Canada abandoned its explicitly ethnocentric and implicitly racist "preferred country" immigration policies in 1963, immigration from other countries in the Western Hemisphere and elsewhere, particularly Asia, began to surge.

Caribbean and Latin American Immigration

Caribbean and Latin American migrants have become the second largest group (after Asians) of non-European immigration to Canada. Flows from Latin America and the Caribbean have been sizable: approximately 20,000 per year over the 1985-1990 period, or about 15 percent of all immigrants to Canada. In the period from 1966 to 1990, some 238,000 migrants came to Canada from the Caribbean, and approximately 128,000 came from Latin America. These immigrants — like all other recent immigrants to Canada — have settled overwhelmingly in three cities — Toronto, Montreal, and Vancouver — and have had a significant impact on the ethnic mix in these locations.

The majority of Caribbean and Latin American migrants to Canada originate in a small number of countries. Virtually all Caribbean migrants come from Anglophone nations, principally Jamaica, Trinidad, and Guyana, although many also come from small Eastern Caribbean islands. There is also a moderate flow from Haiti. Few emigrants from other countries, even very populous ones such as the Dominican Republic, choose Canada as their destination.

The great bulk of Latin American immigrants to Canada have come from a few countries, such as El Salvador and Chile, in the recent past. Smaller but still significant numbers have arrived from Argentina, Brazil, Ecuador, Mexico, and Peru.

Corresponding to these country-specific place of origin patterns, migrant linkages are particularly strong to certain countries. About one-fifth of all emigrants from the Anglophone Caribbean in recent decades have gone to Canada, while the great majority go to the United States (Simmons and Plaza 1990). The Canadian share of recent Salvadoran and Nicaraguan emigrants to North America is more difficult to estimate, but the proportion may be similar.

Temporal Trends

The total inflow of LAC immigrants to Canada has followed a cyclical pattern, reflecting circumstances in home countries and Canadian policies. Starting from very low levels in the early 1960s, immigration from both regions rose quickly to peak in the mid-1970s.

Caribbean immigration rose most quickly during this initial wave. In 1974 nearly thirty thousand immigrants arrived from that region. Latin American immigration to Canada rose more slowly and reached much lower levels. In 1975 about ten thousand Latin American migrants arrived in Canada. The initial surge from the Caribbean seems to have resulted from pent-up demand from previous years (individuals who might have moved previously but could not do so because of policy restrictions), the policies of other countries (Britain closed its doors to Commonwealth Caribbean immigration in 1964), and relatively prosperous times in Canada. The initial surge from Latin America seemed to be based more on the movement of Chileans fleeing domestic political turmoil in the early 1970s.

Subsequent to 1975, immigration from both regions declined and stayed at relatively low levels until 1984, when it rose again. This reflected, in part, lower Canadian immigration targets; inflow over this period related to slower economic growth and, finally, recession in the early 1980s.

The rise in total hemispheric migration to Canada from the mid-1980s through 1990 was partly related to rising total Canadian immigration during this period. It was also due to a rise in the share of regional migrants contributing to overall Canadian immigration. The rising share reflected continuing and even deepening economic crises in a number of Caribbean countries and a rising flood of political refugees from El Salvador and other countries in Central America. In this recent period, LAC immigration totals were similar, with both regions providing approximately fifteen thousand immigrants in 1990.

Country-Specific Patterns

The historical trend of immigration to Canada varies widely from one LAC nation to another (Mata 1985; Simmons 1989). Jamaicans clearly predominated in early flows from the Caribbean, but recent flows are more equally composed of migrants from Jamaica, Trinidad and Tobago, and Guyana. Whereas immigration from Chile reached a peak in 1976 and then gradually declined (to rise again slightly just prior to the return to democracy in the late 1980s), Salvadoran immigration remained at very low levels until 1981, then grew dramatically through the end of the decade. In contrast, immigration from Argentina has been more constant, with a range of five hundred to one thousand immigrants per year during the period from 1974 to 1990. Immigration from Haiti has followed a unique cyclical pattern, reflecting its changing patterns of relative domestic political calm and turmoil.

Classes of Migrants

Motivations for migration vary widely as migrants from Latin America come to Canada as independent workers, family members sponsored by previous immigrants (provided they meet certain selection criteria), and refugees. The refugee component is particularly important in migrant streams from Latin America and has also been significant in the inflow from certain Caribbean countries. Some of the refugees are officially selected abroad as meeting asylum require-ments. Others come to Canada as visitors and claim refugee status upon arrival. A rising number of refugee claimants is, in general, an indication that domestic political and economic circumstances are so threatening that many individuals are willing to take considerable risks to move abroad.

Consider a few contrasting cases: Salvadorans have come to Canada predominantly as refugees selected abroad, mostly from camps and settlements in Costa Rica and other neighboring countries, but some come directly from El Salvador. Yet, many Salvadorans have also come as refugee claimants — a particularly large number of claimants arrived in 1987, which corresponded to changes in U.S. policy on undocumented migrants and the threat that individuals in this category would be deported. Chilean migration to Canada has followed a similar pattern, at least with regard to a rapid rise of Chilean claimants in 1987. Chilean refugees first came to Canada in the mid-1970s after the overthrow of the Allende government. Their choice of Canada partially reflected a lack of U.S. receptivity to Chilean refugees and a greater receptivity in Canada.

Argentines have come to Canada primarily as workers and sponsored relatives. The numbers composing these two groups have risen steadily during the 1990s. Yet, surprisingly, in 1988 and again in 1989, large numbers of Argentines also entered Canada as refugee claimants. A similar pattern is evident for Trinidad and Tobago; two thousand eight hundred refugee claimants arrived in Canada during 1988. In both cases, the inflow of claimants reflected economic crises rather than political repression or violence. In other words, under economic crisis conditions when normal channels for emigrating to Canada are not adequate, individuals may claim refugee status simply to leave for more favored destinations. In cases in which the claims of refugee status are clearly false, visas on travelers are imposed by Canadian officials (the case of Trinidad), or a large portion of the claims are simply rejected (the case of Argentina). In either case, flows of such non-qualifying claimants tend to dwindle quickly.

A number of Latin American countries, such as Peru, stand out because immigration to Canada is based on the movement of workers and sponsored relatives, not on refugee flows. Canadian policy does not generally allow for the acceptance of Peruvians as refugees, even though there is widespread violence and armed insurrection in the country. A few Peruvian refugee claimants arrive in Canada, but most come as family-class migrants.

Interpretation

How may we interpret the timing and specific characteristics of emerging migrant and cultural links from the Caribbean and Latin America to Canada? Are these links momentary and passing, or are they likely to endure and expand? What are the future implications of current patterns?

The preceding questions present a major interpretation challenge. International migration is an extremely complex phenomena that is influenced by social, economic, and political relations between nations as well as individual migrant motives and family, community, and cultural linkages that orient and facilitate movement.

Research on LAC migration flows to Canada is at an early stage, and, therefore, many aspects such as those involving migrant motivation, family connections, and cultural-community linkages are not well understood. The following interpretation is, therefore, limited to a "macro-level" approach concerning the evolution of the Western Hemispheric economic and political system. Specific state policies and emerging cultural linkages are examined within this framework.

The Hemispheric System

The Western Hemispheric system may be described as 1) one involving different classes of nations stratified by their economic and political power as well as 2) a set of relationships between these actors. For the sake of simplicity, we may adopt the now commonly used classification of countries into "core," "semi-periphery," and "periphery," on the understanding that these are analytic constructs and that any given country may move from one class to another over time. Relationships between and among these classes of nations are structured by combined political and economic competition resulting in "winners" and "losers" and dominance and subordination.[2] This, in turn, creates the potential for defined migration patterns, specifically, as follows:

1. The United States has been the most powerful core country in the world system during the postwar period and, by extension, the most powerful country in the Western Hemisphere. Relationships between subsidiary actors such as Canada, the Caribbean, and those select Latin American nations that have formed

migration links with Canada, are shaped by their relationship to the core actor. The United States is the main destination of all hemispheric migrants, including emigrants from Canada as well as those from the Caribbean and Latin America (Pellegrino 1987). Limited access to the United States creates "spill over" migration to other countries, such as Canada, although, as this paper argues, this is not the only mechanism generating Caribbean and Latin American migration to Canada.

2. Within the hemispheric system, Canada is a semi-peripheral country, characterized by very high U.S. investment and ownership of resources and industry (more than two-thirds of Canadian industry is owned or controlled by U.S. firms), close U.S. trade and cultural links, an advanced economic development pattern similar to (although weaker than) that of its powerful neighbor to the south, and a "middle power" status in international affairs. Canada is a major destination for hemispheric migrants, but, as a secondary actor within the system, it also experiences emigration of native-born Canadians principally to the United States (Beaujot and Rappak 1987). In this sense, Canada is something of a "way station" — migrants arrive from more peripheral nations in the system, while significant numbers of native-born (and immigrants) depart in turn. For most historical periods, inflow has exceeded outflow by a ratio of approximately two-to-one or more (Beaujot and Rappak 1987).

3. Caribbean and Latin American countries in the hemispheric system have generally been less advantaged economically than Canada. As relatively "peripheral" within the system, they have often faced significant internal social conflict, including that arising when national liberation movements, socialist governments, and local revolutionary forces have questioned the international system and challenged national interest groups allied to the system. State repression and international intervention in the periphery have been part of the system during the past quarter-century. Combined economic and political "crises" in the Caribbean and Latin America in recent decades have created rising pressures for emigration. Migrants move to more favored neighboring countries, for example, from the Eastern Caribbean to Trinidad (at least until the economic downturn in Trinidad began in 1985) or from Central America to Mexico. They also

migrate in large numbers to the United States and in smaller, but substantial, numbers to Canada. Others move further abroad to Europe.

The widening gap in economic growth between the more developed and the less developed nations in the region generates the potential for significant population movements. Consider the evolution of GNP per capita in the region. In 1970 Jamaica had a GNP per capita of $720, or 20 percent of that in Canada. By 1990 Jamaica's GNP per capita had risen to $1260, but this equaled a mere 7 percent of that in Canada at the same time. Other countries in the region experienced similar development failure in the 1980s.

However, a widening economic gap does not explain migration patterns. It only creates the potential for migration. Other factors both spark and sustain migration. Support for these arguments follows two lines of reasoning. First, empirical studies have shown that there is no correlation between measures of national poverty or economic development in origin countries and levels of migration to Canada (Simmons 1989, 1990a). Rather, social, linguistic, and cultural linkages between the origin country and Canada explain the national background of Canadian immigrants in most cases, while political repression and civil war in origin countries explain the refugee component. Second, immigration to Canada is governed by policies reflecting broader nation-building strategies and planning with respect to the size and composition of the labor force (Simmons and Keohane 1992). In the case of emigration from the Anglophone Caribbean, there is no doubt that the flow to Canada was generated in response to labor force demand in Canada for English-speaking workers with the skills that were readily available in the Caribbean (Simmons and Plaza 1990). Conversely, the largest Latin American migration flows to Canada have been refugee-driven.

From the above perspective, hemispheric migration to Canada may be viewed, first and foremost, as the outcome of systemic patterns of economic inequality, differential labor demand, and different levels of social and political conflict and turmoil within the region. While this perspective provides a basis for understanding the most general features of Canada within the context of hemispheric migration, it is not sufficient to answer certain more specific questions. For example, why did Canadian immigration policies change as they did in 1963, and what other changes in policy have favored LAC immigration to Canada? Why is immigration from the Caribbean mostly from Anglophone countries and minimally from Spanish-speaking countries? Why is immigration from Latin America largely from specific, generally small, refugee-producing nations and not from other large poor nations? Answers to these questions require that any interpretative framework also address state policies.

State Policies

Canadian immigration and refugee policies provide an essential explanation for Canada's role in the inter-American system. First, in its struggle to maintain an "advanced middle power" status, the Canadian state has promoted immigration policies favoring relatively large inflows of immigrant workers during periods of economic expansion and more selective inflows of skilled workers, entrepreneurs, and visa workers in periods of economic recession. This policy has had a contingent relationship to hemispheric migration in recent decades. Canada continued to demand labor in the late 1960s, just as immigration from Europe (with a rapidly rising standard of living) began to dry up. At the same time, economic and political upheaval in the Caribbean and Latin America provided the impetus for emigration. Thus, Canada became an increasingly attractive destination. It was relatively affluent, close (at least to the Caribbean and Central America), and had growing communities of West Indians and Latin Americans to assist new migrants.

Second, the Canadian state has developed refugee policies that have been crucial in forming hemispheric migration links, particularly those to Latin America. The origins of Canadian refugee policy are complex, deriving from a mix of cultural sentiments (humanitarian and Christian values), economic self-interest (a historical tradition of accepting refugees with work skills deemed to be useful), and geo-political considerations (similar to those of the United States and other Western powers during the Cold War that gave preference to refugees from the Soviet bloc, Vietnam, and others). This mix of concerns led Canada to apportion approximately 20 percent of the country's total annual immigration allotment for refugees. It also led the state to recognize that refugee-producing situations had been created by political conditions in Chile after the Pinochet coup; by Argentina during the military dictatorship of the late 1970s and early 1980s; and by El Salvador, Nicaragua, and Guatemala (though not Haiti) through-out the 1980s. Canadian refugee policy may thus be viewed as two-sided: it parallels U.S. policy on some major issues, such as the acceptance of communist country-origin but also diverges in some situations, such as viewing and accepting Salvadorans wishing to emigrate as refugees.

Family reunification is the third pillar of Canadian immigration policy. Spouses and dependent children meeting health and security criteria are virtually assured admittance into Canada. Other applicants may get additional points toward access if they have close relatives in Canada. These policies arise from humanitarian values as well as from political pressures from earlier immigrants. They also reflect the power of the ethnic vote in Canadian cities and the desire of political parties to develop policies that are viewed favorably by these communities (Simmons and Keohane 1992). Once in place, family reunification policies tend to promote sponsorship chains, linking pioneering immigrants to more recent arrivals. Thus, migrant bridges based on an initial movement of workers and refugees tend to be perpetuated, even when original conditions promoting movement have weakened.

Overall, one can argue that Canadian immigration policies and practices since 1963 are consistent with the role of a semi-peripheral nation within the Western Hemisphere. Certain policies emphasize the need for skilled workers and are designed to sustain internal development and a relatively privileged position within both the hemisphere and the world at large. Other policies of a humanitarian nature, such as those for refugees and family reunifications, reflect broad national sentiment, while at the same time they address certain pragmatic objectives arising out of the operation of the wider system. It is convenient for a middle power to promote international leadership in the fight against racism and political repression. This promotes the state's stature in international affairs under circumstances in which other sources of leadership (such as economic or geo-political power) are limited. Having accepted both worker immigrants and refugees at one point in time, it is difficult not to address the political demands of these communities with respect to family reunification, particularly in a context where historic national values also favor such policies.

Cultural Linkages

Canada's place within the hemispheric migration system is conditioned significantly by historical and geographic factors affecting cultural linkages. As an English- and French-speaking nation located on the northern edge of the system, with the United States between it and migrant origin nations, Canada had developed weak human and cultural links with the Caribbean and Latin America. The United States, as the dominant economy and with a long history of migration from LAC countries within the hemisphere, continues to be the major destination for emigrants from the southern part of the Western Hemisphere. In this context, it is not surprising that migration from LAC to Canada has not originated evenly from all countries. Instead, migration has originated from the following:

1. The Anglophone Caribbean and, to a lesser extent, from the Francophone elites in Haiti to Quebec: Political and linguistic links to the Commonwealth Caribbean were undoubtedly important in this pattern from these select countries. Other elements must be added: the Commonwealth Caribbean had developed relatively advanced schooling systems; hence, many emigrants from the region had job skills attractive to Canada. The initial movement from the region was fueled by the closing of the doors in Britain to Commonwealth migrants in 1964 and by the demand for English-speaking domestic workers, school teachers, nurses, and other categories of workers in Canada during the 1970s (Hawkins 1991). Francophone emigrants from Haiti found a milieu in Quebec where they could pursue studies and find jobs in their own language, in a country relatively close to home and to Haitian political life.

2. Refugee producing countries in Latin America: Canada initially had no significant "Latin" cultural or linguistic community in Canada to attract Latin American migrants. In contrast, the United States has a very large Latin community, or rather, a series of large Latin communities (of Puerto Ricans, Cubans, Dominicans, Mexicans, and others). Not surprisingly, Latin American migration to Canada emerged under rather exceptional circumstances. Latin Americans began to come to Canada when the reasons for moving became political as well as economic and when U.S. access was either restricted or implied a more uncertain welcome for the migrants.

The first major wave of Latin American migrants to Canada was from Chile in the years following the Pinochet coup in 1973. Those fleeing had been associated with or sympathetic to the Allende government. As supporters of a socialist regime, these asylum seekers were not welcome in the United States. In addition, many of them did not see the United States as a desirable place to go, given their perception of the U.S. Central Intelligence Agency's clandestine role in the collapse of the Allende government. Sympathetic Canadian trade unions and other parties (particularly, the humanitarian and religious lobbies) encouraged the government to admit Chilean refugees. Under these conditions, some seven thousand migrated to Canada. Subsequent refugee waves have been from Central America and have reflected the timing of armed conflict and repression in the region as well as the unwelcoming stance of the United States toward asylum seekers from El Salvador and Guatemala (Aleinikoff 1992; Basok 1990).

Conclusions

Migration and cultural links to Canada from Latin America and the Caribbean are recent and potentially fragile. Several factors could reduce current migration flows, including:

1. Canada's economic performance and demand for immigrant workers. Canada is currently undergoing a massive restructuring in which a significant portion of industrial capacity and employment was created in the post-war period under import-substitution policies. For example, protective tariffs favoring manufacturing are being lost, perhaps permanently. Construction and other labor-intensive activities are in a slump, such that immigration policy is shifting (Borowski, et al. 1993). Banking, high-tech enterprises such as bio-technology, and computer software development are, in contrast, doing very well, although they produce a smaller portion of total employment. Recently, Canada cut back its targets for a wide range of relatively abundant immigrant workers, while it relaxed criteria for accepting professionals in computer engineering and other specialties who are in scarce supply both inside and outside Canada. A continuation of these trends would eventually make it more difficult for LAC citizens to migrate to Canada.

2. The rise of other semi-peripheral nations within the Western Hemisphere. Mexico is currently poised for entry into NAFTA and is expected to undergo considerable expansion of its manufacturing sector during the next few years. Such developments and their

spin-off effects could have a considerable impact on the destination of Central American refugees. While the current prognosis for Brazil, Argentina, and other large countries with considerable manufacturing bases is not extremely favorable, future prospects should not be discounted.

3. An end to political conflict and repression in the region. There are a number of positive signs, such as the Peace Accord in El Salvador, that suggest that we may be entering a new, more peaceful era. If so, refugee and refugee claimant flows should decline.

While the above scenarios point to possible declining LAC migration to Canada, other trends suggest a continuation of past patterns. Despite the recession of the early 1990s, Canada's immigration targets remain high at two hundred fifty thousand individuals per year. The South-North development gap within the Western Hemisphere has not yet begun to diminish. Social and political conflict in some countries of the region is still high. Whether an improvement or a deterioration in the pattern of inequality within the hemisphere finally occurs, it will be reflected in migration trends. In this sense, migration is an indicator of broader shifts in the international system, and, as such, it merits continuing attention.

Notes

[1] Canada is one of three developed nations (the other two are the United States and Australia) which have, as a matter of policy, continued to admit relatively large numbers of international migrants and refugees. In 1989 and again in 1990, Canada received about two hundred thousand immigrants. Approximately 20 percent of immigrants are refugees selected abroad. In addition, since 1987 about thirty thousand individuals have entered Canada as visitors and subsequently claimed refugee status. Most claimants have had their requests approved and remain in Canada. Nearly three-quarters of the immigrants are from Third World nations. Taking all sources of immigrant inflow into account, Canada is the second most important destination (after the United States) of international migrants. About 17 percent of the Canadian population is foreign-born, a figure that is somewhat lower than Australia's but almost twice the level of that in the United States.

[2] For an expanded treatment of these arguments, see Simmons 1989; Portes and Rumbaut 1990; and Cohen 1987.

References

Aleinikoff, T. A. 1992. "United States Refugee Policy: Past, Present and Future." Paper presented at the Conference on Migration, Human Rights and Economic Integration, York University, Toronto (November).

Basok, Tanya. 1990. "Latin American Refugee Movements and the Canadian Response." In *Prospects for Latin America and the Caribbean in the Year 2000,* ed. A.R.M. Ritter. Ottawa: Institute for International Development and Cooperation, University of Ottawa and the Canadian Association of Latin American and Caribbean Studies.

Basok, Tanya, and Alan Simmons. 1993. "A Review of the Politics of Canadian Refugee Selection." In *The International Refugee Crisis: British and Canadian Responses,* ed. Vaughan Robinson. London: MacMillan.

Beaujot, Roderic, and J. Peter Rappak. 1987. *Emigration from Canada: Its Importance and Interpretation.* Ottawa: Working Paper 4, Policy and Program Development, Immigration Branch, Employment and Immigration Canada.

Borowski, Alan, et al. Forthcoming 1993. "International Movement of Peoples." In *Immigration and Refugee Policy: The Australian and Canadian Experiences,* ed. Howard Adelman. Toronto: York Lanes Press, York University.

Cohen, Robin. 1987. *The New Helots: Migrants in the International Division of Labour.* Brookfield: Gower.

Dirks, Gerry. 1977. *Canada's Refugee Policy: Indifference or Opportunism?* Montreal and Kingston: McGill-Queen's University Press.

Hawkins, Freida. 1991 (2nd ed.). *Critical Years in Immigration: Canada and Australia Compared.* Kingston and Montreal: McGill-Queen's University Press.

Knowles, Valerie. 1992. *Strangers at Our Gates: Canadian Immigration and Immigration Policy, 1540-1990.* Toronto and Oxford: Dundurn.

Mata, Fernando. 1985. "Latin American Immigration to Canada: Some Reflections on the Statistics." *Canadian Journal of Latin American and Caribbean Studies,* X:20, 27-42.

Pellegrino, Adela. 1987. *Migración Internacional de Latinoamericanos en las Américas.* Santiago, Chile: Centro Latinoamericano de Demografía.

Portes, Alejandro, and Ruben Rumbaut. 1990. *Immigrant America: A Portrait.* Berkeley: University of California.

Simmons, Alan. 1989. "World System-Linkages and Internal Migration: New Directions in Theory and Method, with an Application to Canada." *Proceedings of the International Population Conference, New Delhi.* Liege, Belgium: International Union for the Scientific Study of Population.

Simmons, Alan. 1990. "The Origin and Characteristics of 'New Wave' Canadian Immigrants." In *Ethnic Demography: Canadian Immigrant, Racial and Cultural Variation,* eds. S.S. Halli and F. Trovato. Ottawa: Carleton University Press.

Simmons, Alan. 1990a. "Trends and Underlying Forces in Latin American Immigration to Canada." In *Prospects for Latin America and the Caribbean to the Year 2000: Proceedings of a Consultative Symposium,* ed. A.R.M. Ritter. Ottawa: Institute for International Development and Cooperation, University of Ottawa, and the Canadian Association of Latin American and Caribbean Studies.

Simmons, Alan, and Kieran Keohane. 1992. "Canadian Immigration Policy: State Strategies and the Quest for Legitimacy." *Canadian Review of Sociology and Anthropology,* 29:422-452.

Simmons, Alan, and Dwaine Plaza. 1990. "International Migration and Schooling in the Eastern Caribbean." *La Educación* III.

Chapter IV

CANADA'S PROVINCES AND RELATIONS WITH LATIN AMERICA: QUEBEC, ALBERTA, AND ONTARIO

Gordon Mace

The process of province-building in Canada is almost as old as the Confederation itself. It is a process that essentially has come to mean a drive to expand the powers of provincial governments, sometimes by direct confrontation with the federal state (Black and Cairns 1968; Stevenson 1979; Pratt and Richards 1979; Nelles 1974; Chandler and Chandler 1979). Although this expansion of provincial powers has taken different forms depending on the region and type of government involved, mainly it has dealt with the occupation of territory, development of land, transformation of natural resources, and use of those resources to foster industrial development. In some circles, it has been proposed that province-building was also an outgrowth of provincial governments' desire to foster local business elites who felt the federal state was not responsive enough to their particular needs (Pratt and Richards 1979; MacPherson 1968).

Until the 1960s and 1970s, province-building in Canada was mainly an internal phenomenon. Previously, provincial governments were not preoccupied by events outside Canada. By the 1970s, however, they had become more attentive to transformations in the world system as they began to understand how these transformations increasingly affected their own development. From this point on, province-building became a process in which the international dimension continued to grow.

Naturally, the international involvement of Canadian provinces varies considerably from one province to another. Today, the provinces most active in international affairs are Quebec, Alberta, and

---

Gordon Mace is with the Université Laval, Quebec.

Ontario. Since for each of these provinces external relations became an instrument of economic development, an active presence in the United States, Europe, and Asia came to be an important prerequisite in the search for foreign investment and markets for provincial products. For Quebec, the protection and promotion of its particular culture was another important dimension.

This paper examines the external relations of Quebec, Alberta, and Ontario by first presenting an overview of their external relations in Latin America. It compares the behavior of Quebec and Ottawa in the region over the past twenty years and then attempts an evaluation of the successes and failures of Quebec's action in LAC. Finally, it assesses the future of provincial foreign relations within the Western Hemisphere in light of major developments that have occurred in the Americas and elsewhere in the world system.

Quebec, Alberta, and Ontario in Latin America

What has been labeled the "Quiet Revolution" of Quebec society was, in fact, a global process of modernization that has affected all parts of Quebec since the 1960s. Since the election of the Jean Lesage government in 1960, no society in the industrialized world has witnessed so profound a change in such a short period of time (Hamelin 1977). An important element of this process, as well as of the process of province-building, was the need to emerge immediately on the international scene. From this point forward, Quebec's external relations were seen as an important part of an overall strategy to protect and promote the distinctiveness of Quebec society in North America.[1]

Although Quebec was not completely absent from the international scene before 1960, it can be said justifiably that the ongoing process of the province's implication in international affairs really began in the 1960s. The Department of Intergovernmental Affairs was established in 1967 with the mandate of coordinating Quebec's external relations. At that time the main targets of Quebec's international activity were the United States, France, and, to a lesser extent, the United Kingdom. Due to Quebec's geographic proximity to and economic links with the United States, and because of the historical relationship of the two major components of Quebec's population with France and the British Isles, these countries were and continue to be natural objects of Quebec's attention in international affairs.

Very rapidly, however, Quebec began to diversify and extend its external relations first with other partners in Europe and then with countries in Africa, Asia, and Latin America. Today, Quebec has twenty-six offices ranging from bureaus to general delegations spread all over the world.[2] The Department of Intergovernmental Affairs was reorganized in 1984 and became the Department of International Relations. Since 1988 the new Department of International Relations has coordinated Qubec's relations with more than seventy countries. It is quite evident that Quebec's involvement in international affairs will grow at a steady pace in the future, given the increasing complexity of the world system and its ever-growing impact on the province's domestic economy.

With respect to the Americas, Quebec's major trading partner is, of course, the United States, particularly the Northeast, Southeast, and Midwest regions. Approximately 80 percent of Quebec's foreign trade is with the United States, as is 40 percent of investment. Quebec has general delegations in New York, Atlanta, Boston, Chicago, and Los Angeles and other types of representation in Lafayette, North Carolina, and Washington, D.C. In addition, Quebeckers have a strong attachment to the United States and the American way of life, resulting from a very old relationship between the people of Quebec and their counterparts in the Eastern United States (Hero and Daneau 1984; Lublin 1986; Hero and Balthazar 1988; Chodos and Hamovitch 1992).

Quebec's Latin American links are naturally not as strong and diversified as those existing with the United States. However, the relationship between Quebec society and LAC is also very old, going back to the end of the nineteenth century when Catholic priests and nuns from Quebec began establishing missions in different parts of Latin America (Gay 1985). They were followed by business people from Quebec, giving rise to a movement in the 1940s put forward by l'Action Nationale. The movement for the "Union des Latins d'Amérique" was essentially a device through which Quebec and Latin America would have joined forces to counter the influence of the stronger Anglo-Saxon block of North America.[3] While nothing came of this proposal, it established a relationship between the peoples of Quebec and Latin America which was nurtured by immigration, the presence of Latin American students in Quebec, and the creation of friendly cultural associations.

However, intergovernmental relations only began in the latter part of the 1970s with the first government of the Parti Québécois, making the province somewhat of a latecomer in Latin America. It is true that a Quebec bureau was established in Haiti in 1974, but the bulk of Quebec's governmental activity in Latin America actually started between 1977 and 1980. It was during this time, in fact, that a small division on LAC affairs was created within the Department of Intergovernmental Affairs, and delegations were opened in Buenos Aires (1977)[4] and Caracas (1979). They were followed in 1980 by the establishment of a general delegation in Mexico.

During the period from 1977 to 1981, three countries were identified as main targets of Quebec's external relations in Latin America: Haiti, because of the Francophone link; Venezuela, as an important oil producer; and Mexico, because of its potential for cooperation and diversified exchanges (Ministère des Affaires Intergouvernementales 1981). Ministerial visits became more important in the region during this period and peaked in 1980-1981. These ministerial visits brought almost immediate results, and in 1980 Quebec signed its first international agreement with a Latin American country. Within the Department of Intergovernmental Affairs, substantial resources were used to support Quebec's action in Latin America, which reached a high point in 1980-1981 when there were twenty-nine foreign officers in the region and 12 percent of total expenditures was used for foreign representations.[5]

Quebec's relations with Latin America continued to expand from 1981 to 1985, the second term of the René Lévesque government. There was a significant increase in international agreements between Quebec and the governments of Latin America as well as a stabilization of ministerial visits, most of which were economic or commercial missions largely concentrated in Mexico and the Andean countries. The number of foreign officers in the region also increased with the 1985 opening of another Quebec delegation in Bogotá. The increase in Quebec's overall activity in Latin America in the first part of the 1980s greatly contributed to Mr. Bernard Landry's personal interest in the region at that time. As First Minister of External Trade and then Minister of External Relations, Bernard Landry was the moving force of Quebec's expansion in Latin America during these years.

By 1985 Quebec's institutional presence in Latin America had reached a plateau. No additional offices have since been opened, and the election of Robert Bourassa's Liberal government signaled a shift in Quebec's external relations' focus from Latin America to Asia. This shift is apparent both in terms of manpower and expenditures, which decreased in relative terms as well as with respect to ministerial visits which increased in Asia in comparison to Latin America. Surprisingly, in contrast to the overall tendency of Quebec's decreasing external relations with Latin America, the number of international agreements formed with Latin American partners continued increasing.

Ontario and Alberta are the only other Canadian provinces significantly involved in international affairs.[6] Ontario, the most populous and industrialized Canadian province, was well aware of the importance of its presence on the international scene. As such, the Ontario government regularly sent missions outside Canada long before the Confederation was formed: In the 1970s Ontario had nearly fifteen offices spread throughout Europe, the United States, Asia, and Latin America.

Nevertheless, Ontario has always been well served by the Canadian federation system. Its location in the Canadian economy never fueled the perception, as was often the case with Quebec and Alberta, that Canadian foreign policy did not satisfy its interests. The Ontario government did not feel the need to establish a Department of International Affairs. Instead, the management of international activities is divided among various departments, the most important being the Treasury Board, the Department of Intergovernmental Affairs, and the Department of Industry, Trade, and Technology. In 1977 the government of Ontario complied with federal wishes by reducing its presence on the international scene. After closing eleven of its offices outside Canada, the province was left with no official representation in Latin America (Jacomy-Millette 1989, 90). Today Ontario has approximately ten offices located in Europe, the United States, and Asia.

It appears that Latin America is not significantly important to the government of Ontario. As previously mentioned, Ontario closed its offices in Mexico and São Paulo in 1977, and although the Department of Industry, Trade, and Technology continues to send missions to the region, its financing and number of missions decreased during the 1980s in comparison to expenditures for similar missions to the United States and Asia. In the last few years, the government of Ontario has begun to place more importance on its involvement in international affairs. It appears, however, that the role of the province in this area will be concentrated mostly on the United States with generally little interest in Latin America. However, Mexico's importance should increase due to the impact of NAFTA on Ontario's economy, particularly the automobile sector.

The province of Alberta has a status in the Canadian federation that resembles that of Quebec more than of Ontario. Similar to Quebec, although with notable differences, the province of Alberta historically has felt neglected by Ottawa. Successive governments in Edmonton publicly aired their opinion that Ottawa was not interested in the affairs of the province. In addition, when Ottawa's attention was focused on Alberta, there were negative results, such as the New Energy Policy adopted at the end of the 1970s.

The sentiment that federal policies provided greater benefits to the central provinces contributes to the ongoing success of Western-based political movements, such as the Social Credit, the Cooperative Commonwealth Federation (CCF), and, more recently, the Reform Party. It also explains why, in the field of international affairs, Edmonton pursued a policy not altogether different from that of Quebec (Liebich 1982).

In fact, Alberta was the second province after Quebec to establish a Department of Federal and Intergovernmental Affairs. Created in 1972, the department established its International Division in 1978, a division responsible for the coordination of Alberta's international activities and acting liaison with federal departments on matters of international affairs (Statutes of Alberta c.33). In 1979 the government of Alberta named a Minister of International Trade, and today the province has a network of six offices located in London, Tokyo, Hong Kong, New York, Houston, and Los Angeles. Alberta's geographical targets are mainly the United States and Asia with which Edmonton is involved in matters of trade and energy.

With regard to Latin America, the government of Alberta adopted an approach quite different from the one used by Quebec. Until recently, contact with the region was managed through two major channels. The most important was a policy of support for cooperative programs initiated by Alberta's educational institutions with counterparts in Mexico and South America. The other channel was through the Alberta Oil Sands Technology and Research Authority, which has joint programs of development and exchange of energy-related technology with Argentina, Peru, Venezuela, and Brazil. In addition, Alberta has a small international assistance program whose main LAC beneficiaries in 1987 and 1988 were Nicaragua, Peru, Honduras, and Haiti (Alberta, Federal, and Intergovernmental Affairs 1989).

With only about 3 percent of Alberta's exports going to Latin America (mainly Mexico, Brazil, and Cuba), LAC is clearly not a major international affairs partner. This is why, until now, the government of Alberta had never seriously considered the idea of establishing an office in the region. Nevertheless, although Edmonton will continue to emphasize U.S. and Asian relations, it will want to increase its visibility in Latin America in the coming years, particularly if NAFTA and EAI succeed.

A Comparison of Ottawa and Quebec's Behavior Toward Latin America

Formal Canadian relations with Latin America are limited to essentially two governmental actors: Ottawa and Quebec. The following section describes how these governments have managed their relations with the region and what form of coordination has existed between the two. It also compares the policies of both governments in the region.

It is not always easy to assess the level of contact between federal and provincial civil servants posted in cities outside Canada. Insofar as Latin America is concerned, however, there appears to be very little coordination between federal and provincial officials in international affairs. Given this situation, it is somewhat surprising to note the similar behavior of both Quebec and Ottawa in their management of external relations within the hemisphere.

To understand the situation better, let us review briefly the overall trends in Canada's relations with LAC. It is fair to say that until 1970 Canada had little interest in Latin American affairs. During the first hundred years of Canada's existence, Canadian federal government trade missions to the region achieved no significant results. These missions were always sent when Canada's traditional U.S. or European markets were threatened, and, as soon as these trading relations resumed, Canada rapidly forgot Latin America. The brief diplomatic openings of the 1940s had much more to do with the Second World War than with any genuine interest in Latin America. Canada's "benign neglect" was, therefore, the normal state of affairs in its relations with Latin America until the end of the 1960s.[7]

The real beginning of the Canada-Latin America relationship followed a very important 1968 ministerial visit to the region, headed by Secretary of State for External Affairs, Mitchell Sharp. This mission's briefing substantially contributed to the 1970 White Paper that launched Canada's new foreign policy.[8] The White Paper, which brought about substantial changes in the management and the conduct of Canada's external relations, was the result of one of the largest review processes of Canadian foreign policy. Six main issue areas were identified, and emphasis was placed on bilateral relations and the pursuit of Canada's national interests. The White Paper was completed in 1972 with the "Options Paper," which dealt specifically with Canada-U.S. relations (Sharp 1972). In this "Options Paper," the Third Option strategy announced a new Canadian external relations policy of diversification in order to reduce its dependence on the United States.[9]

With regard to Latin America, the 1970 White Paper signaled a new beginning for Canadian relations with the countries of the Western Hemisphere. Soon afterward, Canada became a formal member of the Inter-American Development Bank and, with its observer status at the OAS, became a member of some of its specialized agencies. Canada also became involved financially with CARICOM and the Andean Pact, and the federal government established joint commissions with Mexico, Brazil, and Venezuela. Throughout the 1970s, Latin American countries were the main beneficiaries of most of the governmental programs included in the Third Option strategy. It was clear that Mexico, Brazil, and Venezuela were to form the foundation for the construction of Canada's regional foreign policy.

The final years of the 1980s were a period in which Canada decreased its involvement in Latin America. Essentially, this was a result of economic problems affecting both Canada and Latin America as well as the perception within government circles that Canada's future was increasingly linked to the United States. The Canada-U.S. sectoral trade agreements of 1982 were the first step toward greater linkages that ultimately led to the CUSFTA.

However, Latin America was not completely forgotten despite the attraction of the U.S. market and Canada's growing relationship with Asia. By the mid-1980s, Canada's attention returned to Latin America. Soon after the 1984 election of Canada's Progressive Conservative party, the federal government became involved in the Central American crisis (Rochlin 1988; Lemco 1991). After a slow start, Mr. Clark's successful management of Canada's intervention in the region became a highlight of the government's LAC foreign policy. More important than the crisis in Central America, however, was the recognition by the federal government that the world system was undergoing a profound transformation, leading to a global economy dominated by major trading blocs. Within this new environment, Canada's dominant system of action could only be the Americas, which is why Canada finally agreed to join the OAS as a full member, heralding a new policy toward Latin America (Clark 1990).

In comparing Quebec's behavior in Latin America to Ottawa's, we find a similar overall pattern of relations, albeit with slight differences. Essentially, both governments have been preoccupied with economic opportunities in Latin America during the past twenty years. Ottawa, undoubtedly, has taken a stand on political issues from time to time, but both the federal and provincial governments have been interested primarily in matters of trade, investment, and general cooperation with countries in the region. When looking at behavior patterns over time, similarities are clear, with Quebec experiencing a six- to seven-year lag behind Ottawa. The provincial government became involved in LAC in the early 1970s, five or six years after Canada's first real push in the region. Quebec kept a high profile, while Ottawa became more aloof in its relationship during the early 1980s. Finally, as Ottawa appeared to be renewing relations with Latin America in the latter part of the 1980s, Quebec became less involved. If this pattern holds, Quebec could resume its LAC ties during the next few years, and, later, there should be an expansion of both governments' foreign relations with Latin American partners in the remaining part of the 1990s.

In terms of geographic links, both governments' behavior patterns are similar, although with one significant difference. The two governments have chosen Mexico and Venezuela as their main LAC partners. Quebec has a general delegation in Mexico and a delegation in Caracas, and in the early 1980s Ottawa made Mexico the cornerstone of its Latin American foreign policy. Although seemingly natural choices because of historical relations with these two countries and their national oil resources, Mexico and Venezuela may not be the best choices within the context of overall Canada-LAC relations.

While Brazil has been a major partner for Ottawa, relations with Quebec have been negligible. It is true that at the end of the 1980s, the Quebec government showed a certain interest in Brazil; however, there is still no delegation from the province there, and few formal links are maintained. This is quite surprising given Brazil's importance in Latin America and the fact that in 1990 Brazil was the province's most important commercial partner in the region. A possible explanation for the lack of strong Canadian-Brazilian links might be that few people at the Department of International Affairs are acquainted with Brazil. In addition, many civil servants in the Latin America and Caribbean Division are former missionaries with field work experience in Spanish-speaking Latin American countries. This familiarity with particular Spanish-speaking countries of the region, such as Venezuela, may have influenced Quebec's choice of Latin American partners as well as the location of its delegations. Given Brazil's importance, however, it is expected that stronger ties will be established during the next few years.

Successes and Failures in Provincial Relations with Latin America

Evaluation of these successes and failures is not easy, as no complete survey has ever been made of provincial transactions with LAC countries, and the region has never been a major target of international affairs for Ontario or Alberta. One exception is a fairly large network that has been established in the field of scientific cooperation between Alberta's universities and various Latin American institutions. This network is organized through Alberta's Oil Sands Technology and Research Authority and is strongly supported by the government of Alberta, which also provides technical cooperation to South American countries involved in oil exploration and recovery. In addition, Alberta has been fairly successful exporting wheat, canula, sulphur, and coal to Brazil, Mexico, Cuba, Venezuela, Chile, and Colombia during the past few years (Ministère des Affaires Intergouvernementales 1981). Edmonton hopes that in the future Alberta will successfully promote its products, equipment, and consulting services to Latin America's energy and agricultural industries.

The Canadian province most involved in Latin America is, of course, Quebec. As previously mentioned, Quebec now has four LAC representative offices and has concluded more than twenty international agreements with Latin American countries. The province's major LAC trading partners are Brazil, Mexico, Venezuela, Colombia, Chile, and Jamaica, which accounted for 4.5 percent of all Quebec imports and 2.6 percent of its exports in 1990. The main products exported were airplanes, airplane motors and parts, paper, farm products, and asbestos.

One of Quebec's major successes in Latin America has been in the field of scientific cooperation through inter-university cooperative agreements. In this area Quebec relies heavily on the Inter-American Organization for Higher Education, which groups together university principals from Quebec and Latin America. Quebec has also been successful in attracting students from Latin America to study in the province's universities.

The Quebec business community has had some success in the fields of agro-industry, mass transportation equipment, telecommunications, and the development of human resources. Main players include Northern Telecom and Bombardier, the latter having recently been awarded a contract for Mexico's state-owned Constructora Nacional de Carros de Ferrocarril S.A. (*Globe and Mail* 1992). From the government's point of view, Quebec's hopes for economic gains lie in the fields of energy, mines and geomatics, environment, telecommunications, forestry, and information technologies.

Commercial trends, however, show that all has not been successful. In relative terms, Latin America's share of Quebec's exports has gone from 5.1 percent in 1980 to 2.6 percent in 1990. A similar trend can be observed for Europe, Africa, the Middle East, and, to a lesser extent, the Asia-Pacific region. This situation prompted the Quebec government to issue a recent policy paper on international economic policy (Gouvernement du Québec 1991). Written in close consultation with the business community, the document stresses the need for Quebec to improve its position in foreign markets. Measures suggested included the upgrading of some Quebec bureaus, notably in Venezuela and Colombia; the establishment of a new export market development program; the creation within the Department of International Affairs of a special team to investigate foreign investment prospects; and establishment of a new scholarship program to encourage university-business exchanges in strategic sectors. The document identifies five major Latin American targets: Mexico, Venezuela, Colombia, Brazil, and Chile. Particular attention is paid to the expansion of links with Brazil.

Assessment of Future Trends in Provincial Relations with Latin America

It appears that Canada has made a decision to increase its presence in the Americas. This major reorientation of Canada's foreign policy began with the signing of the CUSFTA, the decision to join NAFTA negotiations, Canada's membership in the OAS, and the announcement of a new Canadian foreign policy toward Latin America. As Mr. Clark said in 1990, Canada has made the decision to "find a home in the Americas," which naturally leads one to question the implications of this new environment on future provincial relations with Latin America.

It is clear that for all Canadian provinces the main actor and the main market in the Americas will continue to be the United States. Therefore, the provinces' attention and international activities in the hemisphere will continue to focus mainly on the United States, and an increase in economic and other transactions along a North-South axis is expected. For example, there is a very strong Quebec presence in New York, New England, and along the entire eastern U.S. coastline. Overall, Canadian presence in the United States should increase in the future, creating large economic regions whose national boundaries will decrease in importance.

A second major trend will be a strengthening of relationships between the large Canadian provinces and Mexico. The recent move by Bombardier is just the latest example of how Canadian businesses will work to establish a presence in Mexico to benefit from lower wages and economic opportunities created by new Mexican policies. Provincial governments will have to follow Quebec's lead and establish more formal links with Mexican federal and state governments in order to encourage further the development of business links. A strong Canada-Mexico relationship will be essential to counterbalance the dominant U.S. position in the North American economy.

Other parts of Latin America will also become more important to the provinces of Quebec, Alberta, and Ontario. Aside from political or security matters, the provinces should see increased business transactions and various forms of cooperative agreements in education, health, culture, and science with the larger LAC countries. All, of course, will depend on the ability of Latin American governments to maintain democratic institutions and an openness to business.

From the Canadian point of view, the country is in a new ball game with respect to inter-American affairs. The region will become Canada's dominant subsystem from which a vast array of significant opportunities will arise. Simultaneously, this new environment will also present important challenges including the management of federal-provincial relations. This factor was not critical when Latin America was peripheral to Canadian foreign policy, but as the relationship becomes more profound and the provinces' international activities increase, there will be a need to coordinate federal and provincial external relations better.

Finally, the provinces themselves will have to improve coordination of their external relations. Improved linkages will be necessary to strengthen mechanisms for local industrial development as well as to create the instruments for promoting external relations.

Notes

[1] On this particular aspect, see Paul Painchaud, 1980, "L'État du Québec et le Systeme International," in eds. Gérard Hervouet and Réjean Pelletier, *L'État du Québec en devenir* (Montréal: Boréal Express), 353-54. See also papers by Painchaud and Latouche, 1988, in eds. I. D. Duchacek, D. Latouche, and G. Stevenson, *Perforated Sovereignties and International Relations* (New York: Greenwood Press).

[2] For a complete list of these offices, see Gouvernement du Québec, 1991, *Le Québec et l'interdépendence: Le monde pour horizon* (Québec: Ministère des Affaires internationales), 127.

[3] On this particular point, see Iris S. Podia, 1948, "Pan American Sentiment in French Canada," *International Journal*, III (Autumn), 331-49.

[4] This delegation was later closed.

[5] The data on Quebec's external relations are taken from an on-going research project at the Centre québecois de relations internationales at Laval University. A more in-depth treatment of Quebec's international activities for the period 1960-1988 appears in Balthazar, Louis, Louis Belanger, and Gordon Mace. 1993. *Trente ans de politique exterieure du Québec* (Sillery, Quebec: Septeritrion).

[6] British Columbia and New Brunswick are also involved in international affairs but on a much smaller scale than Quebec, Ontario, and Alberta. See, for example, Tom Keating and Don Munton, eds., 1985, *The Provinces and Canadian Foreign Policy* (Toronto: Canadian Institute of International Affairs); and A. Jacomy-Millette, 1989, "Les activités internationales des provinces canadiennes," in ed. Paul Painchaud, *De MacKenzie King à Pierre Trudeau: Quarante ans de diplomatie canadienne* (Québec: Presses de l'Université Laval), 81-104.

[7] For an excellent analysis of this period, see, among others, J. C. M. Ogelsby, 1976, *Gringos from the Far North* (Toronto: MacMillan) and David R. Murray, 1974, "Canada's First Diplomatic Missions in Latin America," *Journal of Interamerican Studies and World Affairs*, 16:2, 154.

[8] For more information, see the Government of Canada's 1970 *Foreign Policy for Canadians* (Ottawa: Queen's Printer for Canada).

[9] The Third Option strategy was comprehensive with a local as well as a foreign component. On the domestic front, the strategy implied a restructuring of the Canadian economy by, among other measures, a larger control over foreign investment and an industrial strategy. In the foreign policy field the Third Option was to favor the diversification of Canada's external relations. For an analysis of the latter aspect, see Gordon Mace and Gérard Hervouet, 1989, "Canada's Third Option: A Complete Failure?" in *Canadian Public Policy*, XV:4, 387-404.

References

Alberta, Federal, and Intergovernmental Affairs. 1989. *Fifteenth Annual Report*. Edmonton: Government of Alberta.

Black, Edwin, and Alain Cairns. 1968. "A Different Perspective on Canadian Federalism." In *Canadian Federalism: Myth or Reality*, ed. J. Peter Mackinson. Toronto: Methuen.

"Bombardier Expands Into Mexico." 1992. *The Globe and Mail*. April 10.

Chandler, Marsha, and William M. Chandler. 1979. *Public Policy and Provincial Politics*. Toronto: McGraw-Hill-Ryerson.

Clark, Joseph. 1990. "Notes pour une allocution du très honorable Joe Clark, secrétaire d'Etat aux Affaires Extérieures, à l'Université de Calgary, sur la politique du Canada vis-à-vis de l'Amerique Latine." *Déclarations et Discours* 90:2.

Chodos, Robert, and Eric Hamovitch. 1992. *Quebec and the American Dream*. Toronto: *Between The Lines*.

Duchacek, Ivo, Daniel Latouche, and Garth Stevenson, eds. 1988. *Perforated Sovereignties and International Relations*. New York: Greenwood Press.

Gay, Daniel. 1985. "La présence du Québec en Amérique latine." *Politique* 7:35-52 (Winter).

Gouvernement du Québec. 1991. *Le Québec et l'Interdépendence: Le monde pour horizon*. Québec: Ministère des Affaires Internationales.

Government of Canada. 1970. *Foreign Policy For Canadians*. Ottawa: Queen's Printer.

Hamelin, Jean. 1977. *Histoire du Québec*. Toulouse: Privat.

Hero, Jr., Alfred O., and Marcel Daneau, eds. 1984. *Problems and Opportunities in U.S.-Quebec Relations*. Boulder: Westview Press.

Hero, Jr., Alfred O., and Louis Balthazar. 1988. *Contemporary Quebec and the United States, 1980-1985*. Lanham: University Press of America.

Jacomy-Millette, Anne-Marie. 1989. "Les activités internationales des provinces canadiennes." In *De MacKenzie King à Pierre Trudeau: Quarante ans de diplomatie canadienne*, ed. Paul Painchaud. Québec: Presses de l'Université Laval.

Keating, Tom, and Don Munton, eds. 1985. *The Provinces and Canadian Foreign Policy.* Toronto: Canadian Institute of International Affairs.

Lemco, Jonathan. 1991. *Canada and the Crisis in Central America.* New York: Praeger Publishers.

Liebich, Christopher. 1982. *Provinces Abroad: Alberta and Quebec Confront Ottawa. Two Models of Provincial Behavior in External Affairs.* Ottawa: Carleton University, Department of Political Science, unpublished research essay.

Lublin, Martin. 1986. "Quebec-U.S. Relations: An Overview." *American Review of Canadian Studies,* 16:1 (Fall).

MacPherson, C. B. 1968. *Democracy in Alberta: Social Credit and the Party System.* Toronto: University of Toronto Press.

Mace, Gordon, and Gérard Hervouet. 1989. "Canada's Third Option: A Complete Failure?" *Canadian Public Policy,* XV:4 (December).

Ministère des Affaires Intergouvernementales. 1981. *Report annuel 1979-1980.* Québec: Éditeur officiel du Québec.

Murray, David R. 1974. "Canada's First Diplomatic Missions in Latin America." *Journal of Interamerican Studies and World Affairs,* 16:2 (May).

Nelles, H. V. 1974. Politics of *Development.* Toronto: MacMillan.

Ogelsby, J. C. M. 1976. *Gringos From the Far North: Essays in the History of Canadian-Latin American Relations 1866-1968.* Toronto: MacMillan Publishers.

Painchaud, Paul. 1980. "L'État du Québec et le systeme international." In *L'État du Québec en devenir,* eds. Gérard Hervouet and Réjean Pelletier. Montréal: Boréal Express.

Podia, Iris S. 1948. "Pan American Sentiment in French Canada." *International Journal,* III (Autumn).

Pratt, Larry, and John Richards. 1979. *Prairie Capitalism: Power and Influence in the New West.* Toronto: McClelland and Stewart.

Rochlin, James. 1988. "The Political Economy of Canadian Relations with Central America." *Canadian Journal of Latin American and Caribbean Studies,* 13:25.

Sharp, Mitchell. 1972. "Canada-U.S. Relations: Options for the Future." *International Perspectives* (Autumn).

Statutes of Alberta. The Department of Federal and Intergovernmental Affairs Act. C. 33.

Stevenson, Garth. 1979. *Unfulfilled Union*. Toronto: Gage.

Chapter V

FOREIGN POLICY AND CANADA'S EVOLVING RELATIONS WITH THE CARIBBEAN COMMONWEALTH COUNTRIES: POLITICAL AND ECONOMIC CONSIDERATIONS

Gregory S. Mahler

The Canadian Foreign Policy Setting: Foreign Policy Eras

Canadian foreign policy since World War II can be described as chronologically composed of four distinct eras, made up of two periods based upon different thematic bases, with two corresponding periods of transition into and out of these specific eras. The first period is "liberal internationalism" and occupied the period from 1945 to the early 1960s. This was followed by a transitional period in the 1960s, often referred to as "Canadian nationalism." This transitional nationalist period led to the third era and the second major thematic approach — conducted during the Trudeau years, it is referred to as Canada's "neo-realist" foreign policy era. Some analysts argue that another transitional period has characterized Canadian foreign policy since 1980, and they describe it as a "marketing of Canadian culture" in countries with which Canada wishes to have trade relations (Cooper 1985; Lyon and Tomlin 1979).

During the era of liberal internationalism, Canada was largely an unselfish actor, playing the role of "mediator" or "peacekeeper" between the superpowers (Lyon and Tomlin 1979). Dewitt and Kirton

Gregory S. Mahler is with the Department of Political Science, University of Mississippi.

have noted that during those years, "Canada pursued the central purpose of steadily constructing a more durable and just international order for all" (1983, 1). Canada's peacekeeping efforts included support for the founding of and participation in the United Nations, advocacy of NATO, and promotion of East-West detente, as well as efforts in "helping the Commonwealth evolve from a largely Anglo-Saxon-dominated group into a loose association of independent states."[1]

During this period, economic strategy was also perceived as a significant component of Canadian foreign policy. This was demonstrated by Canada's advocacy of liberal trading relations as well as its support for economic associations, such as the GATT, the IMF, and the Organization for Economic Cooperation and Development (OECD). Perhaps most important, this era saw "no conflict between Canada's idealistic interna-tionalism and Canadian national interest" (Dewitt and Kirton 1983, 5).

In the 1960s, however, a new school of thought developed, and the growth of Canadian nationalism during this period was responsible for a change in the way Canada thought about the world. It has been argued that this period of Canadian foreign policy provided a link between the liberal internationalist period, which lasted until the 1960s, and Pierre Trudeau's "neo-realism" of the 1980s.

Some scholars have felt that Canada's self-described "middle power" role during the W.L. Mackenzie King, John G. Diefenbaker, and Lester Pearson administrations was based on naiveté. Thus, the net effect of this approach to foreign policy was Canada's legitimization of U.S. aggression around the globe, including the Vietnam war (Lyon and Tomlin 1979). An argument regarding Canadian foreign policy prior to the 1960s posited that Canada had become a dependent and an economic satellite of the United States. Not only were key sectors of the Canadian economy largely American-owned, but, as noted by Doran and Sigler (1985, 5), "U.S. trade policy was conditioned by the broad international environment, while Canadian trade policy was again heavily directed toward the United States."

The early 1960s, then, witnessed a reconsideration of Canadian foreign policy. It was argued that "the closeness that arose from the experience of World War II and the shared responsibilities for building the international institutions in the immediate post-war world have passed" (Doran and Stigler 1985, 3). The nationalism of the 1960s led directly to a major foreign policy review conducted by the Trudeau government that indicated the beginning of a new era for Canadian foreign policy. The review was conducted from 1968 to 1970 and culminated with the report entitled *Foreign Policy For Canadians*.[2] This document and the Third Option policy paper put forth in 1972 by Secretary of State for External Affairs Mitchell Sharp signified a major change in Canada-U.S. relations: Canada would no longer be an unselfish middle power, seeking to effect a harmonious relationship between the superpowers. Rather, the Trudeau doctrine of complex neo-realism portrayed a global Canadian pursuit of defined national interests through the development and management of direct bilateral relationships with carefully selected states (Sharp 1970; Sharp 1972; Dewitt and Kirton 1983).

Not surprisingly, this neo-realist era was perceived as an attempt to reorder the priorities of post-World War II liberal internationalism. In public opinion studies, "peace-keeping" was regarded as the third-ranked goal of Canadian foreign policy after "fostering economic growth" and "safeguarding sovereignty and independence" (Sharp 1970). Another indicator of Canada's reordered priorities was found in the government's attitudes toward U.S. economic influence on Canada. As Mitchell Sharp argued in his 1972 Third Option, the only real strategy for Canada was to seek new trade partners in order to offset U.S. influence. Thus, Canada sought to expand its international relations in a variety of ways.

The fourth era in Canadian foreign policy has developed since 1980 and can be characterized essentially as an extension of the neo-realist doctrine. Marked by an expansion of Canadian foreign policy offensives and focused on making Canada better known in previously ignored areas, the major priority in this fourth era is to enhance the Canadian economy through the establishment of new trade relationships.

These four periods, the "liberal-internationalist," the "nationalist," the "neo-realist I (Pierre Trudeau)," and the "neo-realist II (Brian Mulroney)," describe the evolution of Canadian foreign policy in the post-World War II era.

Canada and the Caribbean

There is a long history of Canadian-Caribbean relations. As long ago as 1884, local legislatures in Barbados, Jamaica, and the Leeward Islands sought to associate their territories formally with Canada. In addition, the Bahamas sought to join the Canadian Confederation, and "as recently as 1974, the State Council of the Turks and Caicos Islands had asked that their territory be annexed by Canada" (Thomas 1988, 338).

Kari Levitt points out in "Canada and the Caribbean: An Assessment," that "Canada did not develop diplomatic relations with the major countries of continental Latin America until the 1970s.... By contrast, it has long historic ties with the Caribbean, most particularly with the Commonwealth Caribbean...;" in fact, the Commonwealth Caribbean "is the area of the Third World with which Canada has the longest and closest ties" (1988, 229). Although the overall trade relationship between Canada and these nations has declined to the point that it is not significant for either Canada or these Caribbean nations, the Commonwealth countries continue to be significant foreign policy entities for Canada. The association with the Commonwealth Caribbean allows Canada to participate in the development process of the hemisphere, to exercise some stabilizing influence on the potentially turbulent politics of the region, and to administer a development assistance program to make a difference in the relatively small economies of the region.

One major dimension of this political relationship was Canada's ambivalence about joining the OAS. The Canadian government described the general arguments in favor of and against joining the organization in *Foreign Policy for Canadians* (1970). While membership would increase Canada's ties with regional governments and help Canada achieve its economic, social, and cultural goals in the hemisphere, the government also suggested that OAS membership might obligate Canada to comply with collective decisions of the body and, at the very least, might restrict Canada's freedom of action with regard to development assistance issues.

> It may be that, at a certain point in time, a Canadian government will conclude that Canada could best foster [its goals for the region] by joining the OAS. In the meantime, Canada should draw closer to individual Latin American countries and to selected inter-American institutions, thus preparing for whatever role it may in the future be called upon to play in the Western Hemisphere and gaining the experience which is indispensable in a complex *milieu* which few Canadians yet know very intimately.[3]

That "certain point in time" came, of course, with Prime Minister Brian Mulroney's 1989 decision for Canada to join the OAS. He believed, along with many others, that Pierre Trudeau's concerns about Canadian sovereignty no longer were valid and that Canada did not need to worry about being committed to the OAS. Further, the feeling of the time was that Canada's role in the region was sufficiently important to justify joining the OAS.

Economic Considerations

Trade

For many years, Canada has been a supporting trade partner with many of the countries of the Commonwealth Caribbean. On a more official level, CIDA is a supporter of the Caribbean Association of Industry and Commerce (Thomas 1988, 33). According to one recent study, although Canada remains an important trading partner for many of these nations, its significance is far less than it was in earlier years. For example, in 1988 Canada was the fifth-largest source of imports to the Bahamas, following the United States, the United Kingdom, the EC, and Japan. It was the third-largest partner for Barbados, following the United Kingdom and the United States (Braveboy-Wagner 1989). Nevertheless, it is clear that Canada's market share of trade with these countries has diminished in recent years (Levitt 1988).

Many Canadian banks and investment companies have long-standing relationships with some Commonwealth Caribbean nations. In particular, the Cayman Islands are favored by Canadian companies as offshore financial centers (Thomas 1988). In addition, not only has "the Caribbean been the principal supplier of bauxite and alumina to the United States and Canada, but its stake in the oil trade is also considerable" (Thomas 1988, 106).

A number of "Canadian" companies are either wholly owned subsidiaries of American interests — for example, Commonwealth Holiday Inns — or have a substantial degree of American investment, such as Alcan. Therefore, American policy does influence Canadian economic behavior in the LAC region. This has led some critics to charge that "under the Mulroney government, Canadian foreign policy is increasingly subsuming a gamut of international relations beneath bilateral U.S./Canada ties" (Thomas 1988, 339).

One of the major issues in Canadian-Caribbean relations in recent years has been the Reagan administration's 1982 Caribbean Basin Initiative (CBI). At the outset, the CBI appeared as though it would help solve many of the region's long-term development and trade problems by promoting 1) duty free entry to the U.S. market for some Caribbean products, 2) tax credits for U.S. businesses investing in the Caribbean, and 3) aid from the United States. However, it became clear after a relatively short period of time that the Reagan administration tied strings to the initiative and "link[ed it] with the U.S. government's military and security interests.... Like the Alliance for Progress in Latin America in the 1960s, it was prompted by Cold War considerations" (Thomas 1988, 337). George Schultz noted from the American point of view, "the Caribbean Basin is vital to our security and to our social and economic well-being" (Thomas 1988, 337).

In fact, however, many of the Commonwealth Caribbean nations did not want to be the "third border" of the United States, and, as CBI was increasingly viewed with skepticism, Caribbean eyes turned to Canada as a possible alternative source of markets and economic assistance. From this situation came the establishment of CARIBCAN in 1986. In many respects, CARIBCAN is similar to the CBI in that, with some exceptions, it permits duty-free trade for products defined as Caribbean-made. This was apparently intended to cover virtually all Canadian imports from the English-speaking Caribbean. Items such as some textiles, clothing, footwear, luggage, and certain others are not included in the blanket duty-free understanding. CARIBCAN also provided for the doubling of Canadian aid between 1982 and 1987 (from approximately US$28.5 million to US$57 million). In addition, since Canada has a smaller regional presence and does not arouse fear about possible big-power ambitions, CARIBCAN was popular with many of the Caribbean nations. Furthermore, CARIBCAN was well designed to meet the needs of the English-speaking Caribbean.

Even if trade is not the primary reason for Canada's continued interest in this region and the overall *proportion* of the Caribbean market controlled by Canadians may have declined over the years, the Canadian presence has been, and continues to be, important in a number of economic realms. For example, Canadian mining interests, manufacturers, financial institutions, and other economic actors continue to operate in the Commonwealth.

Tourism

One of the key aspects of economic relations tying Canada to the Caribbean is tourism.

Over the longer term, the Caribbean's superb resort assets, its warm climate throughout the year, its [reasonably close location]...to the United States and Canada — together with the growth of incomes and scarcity of beaches in those North American countries — will ensure the eventual recovery of demand for tourism in the Caribbean region (Kempe 1986, 49).

Until 1979, Canada was the major tourism-generating country for many of the Commonwealth Caribbean nations (Kempe 1986). To give one example, in 1979 Sun Tours of Canada transported four hundred thousand tourists via three thousand flights to the West Indies which was more than the number of residents of any individual country in the Eastern Caribbean. Since 1980 Canada's position as the primary tourist market was taken over by the United States (Kempe 1986, 150-1). However, Canada continues to provide a major portion of tourists to the region each year (Thomas 1988, 147-51).

Economic Development Assistance

Tourism and residents who originally came to Canada from the Commonwealth Caribbean substantially enhance Canada-Caribbean links. Nevertheless, Canada's primary ties to the Commonwealth Caribbean are at the governmental level, of which a major component is Canada's program of development aid. This program began in 1958 when "the West Indies Federation was launched by London in an effort to dump the burden of supporting a set of colonies that had long since lost their attraction as economic assets" (Levitt 1988, 235). Over the years Canada, along with the United States and the United Kingdom, has been one of the major sources of foreign economic development aid to the Commonwealth Caribbean (Braveboy-Wagner 1989, 83).

Political Considerations

Perceptions of Canada

The perception of Canada in the Caribbean is as a more benign neighbor than the United States. Canadian attitudes toward the region are viewed differently from U.S. attitudes and, thus, so is Canada's potential behavior. Levitt describes this profile:

In the Caribbean, Canada enjoys a favorable image, as much for negative as for positive reasons. It is not a superpower that regards the Caribbean as its third frontier, or as its *mare nostrum*. Nor is Canada a former colonial power, as is Britain, France, or the Netherlands. It has no territorial designs in the Caribbean, as does Venezuela, for example. Together with Mexico, Canada is the only country in the hemisphere that maintained diplomatic relations with Cuba after its revolution. Canada has been respectful of the regional effort of the Commonwealth Caribbean and does not as a rule attach political conditions to development aid— although the commercial strings are very tightly tied (Levitt 1988, 226-7).

Thus, although U.S. aid programs, or programs like CBI, might be welcomed in the Caribbean, these countries are often concerned about the *motives behind*, and possible *implications of*, accepting U.S. aid. U.S. policymakers' speeches about the strategic implications of CBI served to make many Caribbean nations wary of it. The Caribbean appreciated and wanted the economic improvements promised by the Initiative, but they were unhappy about its Cold War and anti-Cuba implications.

Prime Minister Trudeau's 1983 speech in St. Lucia is frequently cited as providing an explanation of *why* Caribbean reactions to Canada are different from those to the United States. Trudeau stated:

We have consistently chosen to address hemispheric tensions from their economic and social causes, being equipped neither by ambition nor by capacity to pursue military solutions, or grand strategic designs. Consequently, we have urged on other partners a developmental approach — national plans and regional institutions. In our view states have a right to follow whatever ideological path their peoples decide. When a country chooses a socialist or even a Marxist path, it does not necessarily buy a "package" which automatically injects it into the Soviet orbit.[4]

Canada has been quite consistent in following this doctrine, and while the Mulroney era may have placed more emphasis on the "selling" of Canada, it has, for the most part, not violated the principles laid down by Prime Minister Trudeau almost a decade ago.

Security Considerations

Canada has regularly been involved in the training of defense forces in the Caribbean. It was involved in training the small Belize Defense Force. In the 1960s and 1970s, Canada (along with Britain) helped to train Guyanese and Jamaican military forces. Also with Britain, it played a role in the training of Trinidad's military forces as well as those of other states in the Eastern Caribbean. According to Braveboy-Wagner, "Canada...continues to play a tertiary role in training and equipping the military and police forces of the Caribbean" (1989, 39).

Accordingly, Canadian support for Commonwealth Caribbean security concerns has been articulated and operationalized differently from that of the United States. The clearest difference between the two is illustrated by their approaches to CBI, which was initially advocated and subsequently interpreted by the Reagan administration to include a security dimension. Canada, on the other hand, initially supported the Initiative and, subsequently, "de facto dissociated" itself from the expanded interpretation of the policy *because of* the new American interpretation of a security dimension (Levitt 1988, 241).

This does not suggest, however, that the Commonwealth Caribbean states have rejected American security assistance. "Both quantitative and qualitative analyses suggest that the United States has increasingly been replacing, or for certain countries equaling, Britain as the main partner for the English-speaking countries in security matters" (Braveboy-Wagner 1989, 54). The "intervention" in Grenada, for example, demonstrated to all concerned that, when circumstances are appropriate, Caribbean leaders quite willingly accept American military and security intervention. In addition, American naval forces regularly pay courtesy calls on Caribbean ports today.

Another major security concern is the drug trade and the relative impotence of small nations to deal with associated problems. At the Sixth Commonwealth Parliamentary Conference held in 1986, the drug trade issue was raised by Barbados' Speaker of the Parliament, who suggested that the problem faced by small island democracies was that they could not afford the equipment necessary for the interdiction of drug traffickers.[5] Among others, legislators from the Bahamas, the Turks and Caicos Islands, St. Vincent, and Grenada have also echoed these complaints, and in recent years they have sought help from the

United States and Canada. Plans for ways to handle the problem are still being developed, but it is clear that Commonwealth Caribbean policymakers see both Canada and the United States as significant actors in its resolution.

Trends and Issues of Emerging Policy Importance

Even if its relationships with other countries of Latin America and the OAS are not well developed, Canada has a well-established history with many countries of the Commonwealth Caribbean. Although the relationship mostly focuses on economic and political issues, commonalities shared in the cultural realm cannot be forgotten. Shared interests include Caribbean immigration to Canada, a common political heritage, and common political institutions, which provide a base upon which political and economic relations can be built. Although in many respects Canada's presence in the Caribbean is second to the United States', Canada *is* a significant actor.

Canada's relative influence has diminished for three basic reasons. First, in recent years Canada — like so many other countries, including the United States — has had domestic budgetary problems. As a result of these restrictions, Canada has not been able to do as much internationally as it might have liked, and aid programs have not been expanded to the degree that many Caribbean and Canadian leaders had wanted.

Second, domestic political issues have distracted Canadian attention from the international horizon. Questions of international relations that previously predominated in the Canadian political arena have clearly taken a back seat to issues of constitutional reform, Quebec's relation with the rest of the federal system, and the future of the Canadian Confederation. Simply put, Meech Lake[6] pushed CARIBCAN out of the public's view; this has resulted in less government attention to related issues.

Third, the political agenda of Brian Mulroney, which placed more emphasis on "selling" Canada, developing international trade, and increasing Canada-U.S. ties, has dictated that Canada not act in a way that might adversely affect this relationship. Accordingly, the Canadian government has been more willing under Mr. Mulroney than under Mr. Trudeau to step back and avoid confrontations with the United States on a variety of foreign issues. This includes those related to the Caribbean.

There still remain a number of basic questions that have yet to be resolved regarding Canadian relations with the Commonwealth Caribbean. In closing, there are many issues that are of policy importance that must be addressed in the future. The following is a general list of issues to be taken into account by Canadian leaders and those of the Commonwealth Caribbean countries:

Economic Issues

- Development of new trade agreements between Canada and the nations of the region and agreements between and among these and other nations.

- Determination of the future of Canadian tourism in the region and ways to increase it.

- Diversification of local economies to lessen the relative impact of single industries, such as tourism, sugar cane, and oil.

- Identification of new developmental aid initiatives that can be undertaken either bilaterally or multilaterally.

Political Issues

- Development of formal relationships between the Caribbean Commonwealth nations and Canada and continuation of discussion of the significance of the Commonwealth as an association.

- Identification of new initiatives that give governments in the region the power to fight and resolve the drug crisis.

- Creation of initiatives to develop the political stability of the regimes of the Commonwealth Caribbean in order to avoid the type of instability that led to the Grenada Revolution.

Notes

1 Charles Doran and John Sigler, eds., 1985, *Canada and the United States: Enduring Friendship, Persistent Stress* (Englewood Cliffs, N.J.: Prentice-Hall). On Canada's role in the Commonwealth, see Ian Grey, 1986, *The Parliamentarians: The History of the Commonwealth Parliamentary Association, 1911-1985* (Cambridge: Gower Publishing Co.). On Canada's relations with Britain, and the degree to which Canadian policy was influenced by Britain, see Norman Hillmer, 1985, "The Canadian Diplomatic Tradition," in ed. Andrew Fenton Cooper, *Canadian Culture* (Toronto: Canadian Institute of International Affairs).

2 This was a six-volume set with individual booklets on Latin America, Europe, the Pacific, the United Nations, International Development, and a general introductory volume to present the major issues. See Mitchell Sharp, 1970, *Foreign Policy for Canadians* (Ottawa: Information Canada).

3 This comes from volume four of the 1970 series *Foreign Policy for Canadians,* entitled "Latin America," 22-24.

4 Remarks by Pierre Trudeau at the Commonwealth - Western Hemisphere Nations Meeting in St. Lucia on February 20, 1983, as cited in Kari Levitt, 1988, "Canada and the Caribbean," in eds. Jorge Heine and Leslie Manigat, *The Caribbean and World Politics: Cross Currents and Cleavages* (New York: Holmes and Meier), 227.

5 This debate, "Drugs: The Social and Economic Implications" took place at the Sixth Commonwealth Parliamentary Conference of Members from Small Legislatures, held in Jersey, Channel Islands, in September 1986. The minutes were subsequently published by the Commonwealth Parliamentary Association, Palace of Westminster, London.

6 The Meech Lake Accord among the federal and provincial governments recognized Quebec as a distinct society. A detailed explanation can be found in Chapter 8 of this volume.

References

Braveboy-Wagner, Jacqueline Anne. 1989. *The Caribbean in World Affairs: The Foreign Policies of the English-Speaking States.* Boulder, Colo.: Westview Press.

Cooper, Andrew Fenton. 1985. *Canadian Culture: International Dimensions.* Toronto: Canadian Institute of International Affairs.

Dewitt, David B., and John J. Kirton. 1983. *Canada as a Principal Power.* Toronto: John Wiley and Sons.

Doran, Charles, and John Sigler. 1985. *Canada and the United States: Enduring Friendship, Persistent Stress.* Englewood Cliffs, N.J.: Prentice Hall.

Grey, Ian. 1986. *The Parliamentarians: The History of the Commonwealth Parliamentary Association, 1911-1985.* Cambridge: Gower Publishing Company.

Hilmer, Norman. 1985. "The Canadian Diplomatic Tradition." In *Canadian Culture: International Dimensions,* ed. Andrew Fenton Cooper. Toronto: Canadian Institute of International Affairs.

Kempe, Ronald Hope. 1986. *Economic Development in the Caribbean.* New York: Praeger.

Levitt, Kari. 1988. "Canada and the Caribbean: An Assessment." In *The Caribbean and World Politics: Cross Currents and Cleavages,* eds. Jorge Heine and Leslie Manigat. New York: Holmes and Meier.

Lyon, Peyton V., and Brian W. Tomlin. 1979. *Canada as an International Actor.* Toronto: MacMillan of Canada.

Sharp, Mitchell. 1972. "Canada-U.S. Relations: Options for the Future." *International Perspectives* (Fall).

Sharp, Mitchell. 1970. *Foreign Policy for Canadians.* Ottawa: Information Canada.

Thomas, Clive. 1988. *The Poor and the Powerless.* New York: Monthly Review Press.

Chapter VI

CANADA AND THE ANDEAN DRUG WARS

James Rochlin

Cocaine trafficking, now considered to be Latin America's largest multinational industry (McClintock 1988), has several important ramifications for Canada both domestically and in terms of Canadian policy interests in South America. These concerns range from the crisis of consumption of crack cocaine in Canada's largest cities to Canada's provision of security assistance to the governments of Colombia and Peru. Ottawa is also particularly concerned with threats to regional security emanating from the drug war that may impede progress toward achieving the EAI. One specific example is the "balloon" effect, through which pressure exerted upon the Andean region to crack down on the narcotics trade causes pressure to spread to neighboring countries, such as Argentina, Brazil, and Venezuela.

The strategic context is especially significant in that the Andean region now receives more U.S. military assistance than any other region in the hemisphere (Andreas 1991-92), creating a situation that some have deemed the "Central Americanization" of the Andean countries. Ottawa, however, is not generally supportive of the U.S. militarization scheme as a means of addressing the problem. Overall, issues of security and economic development as well as social concerns regarding drug addiction contribute to Canadian interest in narcotrafficking and narcoterrorism. Despite the obvious significance of the crisis, scant research has been conducted in this area, particularly from the Canadian perspective.

James Rochlin is a Research Fellow at the Centre for Research on Latin America and the Caribbean, York University. He is also Professor and Chair of the Department of Political Science, Okanagan University College, Kelowna, British Columbia.

The process of hemispheric integration is proceeding rapidly, and Canada is very much a part of it. Developments, such as the North American and Western Hemisphere free trade initiatives, Canada's full membership in the OAS, and the Canadian role in conflict resolution of the Central American imbroglio, are all evidence of the country's recent immersion in hemispheric affairs. Thus, it is incumbent upon Ottawa to take a clear and independent stance in what is obviously the most worrisome strategic issue in the Americas: the Andean drug war.

The central argument here is that the twin crises of narcotrafficking (the transit and marketing of illicit drugs) and narcoterrorism (terrorist activities launched by drug traffickers often in an attempt to gain legitimacy within the system) are rooted in the underdeveloped poverty of the South and the high consumption of the North. This must be recognized when creating effective policies aimed at alleviating the crises, and the best arena for the construction of such policies is within the OAS.

Emphasizing at the outset the empirical limitations inherent in this sort of investigation, this analysis begins with a discussion of the Andean context of the crisis and then turns to a consideration of Canadian policy and interests. Clearly, there are a number of reasons why many figures can be regarded as only rough indicators. It is not surprising, for example, that narcotraffickers do not make a habit of reporting their quarterly profits to local authorities. Hence, analysts must rely on guesswork. There are other considerations as well. For instance, data on the quantity of drugs consumed or exported may reflect the ideological or strategic agenda of those who disseminate such information. Furthermore, the price of exportable cocaine varies according to quality, exchange rate considerations, shifting prices of required processing chemicals, location of transactions, and specula-tion regarding trends in future prices.[1]

In the early 1990s, there were estimated to be 250,000 hectares of land utilized for coca production in Peru, compared with about 27,000 hectares in Colombia and 80,000 hectares in Bolivia. Peru, particularly the Huallaga Valley region, produces the majority of the world's coca leaves that are processed into salable cocaine (*El Spectador* 1990).

Increasingly, final processing occurs in Peru and Bolivia in an effort to demand a higher price for the product.[2] Even when all the processing is done in Peru, the product generally is transported to

Colombia where traffickers determine shipping routes to the North. In Bolivia the recent trend is for the product to travel through Brazil and Argentina enroute to markets in Europe.

Peru and Bolivia

As previously mentioned, production of coca leaves occurs mostly in Peru. There are an estimated sixty thousand to three hundred thousand families residing in Peru's Huallaga Valley that cultivate coca leaves (McClintock 1988, 128). Those families, cultivating one or two hectares, each earned incomes estimated to range upward from US$8,000 annually during the mid-1980s (Tullis 1987). The average annual Peruvian per capita income is US$960 (IMF 1986).

In order to understand the momentum behind the influx of peasant families engaged in coca cultivation in the Huallaga Valley, one must appreciate the devastation of the Peruvian political economy. According to noted Peruvian sociologist Guillermo Rochabrun Silva (1988, 88), the "general context of pauperization" that characterizes Peru explains the attraction of elements of the local population to "the sudden enrichment that the drug trade provides. Therein lies a reasonable explanation of the current levels of demoralization and corruption."

Statistics convey the economic and social misery suffered by Peruvians. Between 1980 and 1985, inflation in Peru was calculated at 3,000 percent annually (Craig 1987), and during the presidency of Alan Garcia (1985-1990), prices rose an incredible 2 million percent (*Globe and Mail* 1990). Inflation, which in 1989 was 2,775 percent, jumped to an astonishing 7,750 percent in 1990 (*Latin American Weekly Report* 1991), and then it simmered down to 139 percent in 1991 after the "Fujishock" which will be discussed shortly (*Latin American Weekly Report* 1992). The average monthly salary of Peruvians, however, remained at US$35 during the early 1990s (Peredes and Sachs 1990). Furthermore, three-quarters of the population are undernourished and either underemployed or unemployed (Craig 1987). In a desperate attempt to survive, approximately 70 percent of the population work in the "informal sector," selling whatever services or products are marketable on the streets.

The austerity measures imposed by newly elected President Fujimori and the IMF in the summer of 1990 were dubbed "Fujishock" by the local media. Restructuring caused a rise in gasoline prices from

US$.13 per gallon to US$4 per gallon, along with an increase in food prices of 400 percent (*Globe and Mail* 1990). In an attempt to suppress anticipated public violence in the wake of the shock, a state of siege was declared in Lima.

Amidst economic devastation, the cocaine industry represents a "safety valve" of survival.[3] The drug, worth about US$1 billion to the Peruvian economy in the early 1990s, is Peru's biggest export (Andreas 1991-2; Lee 1990), representing about 30 percent of the value of the country's total legal exports and comprising 18 percent of its 1987 GDP (Deustua 1987). Production of the narcotic employs roughly 15 percent of the country's work force. Realistic, effective attempts to eradicate coca production in Peru, therefore, must come to grips with the elements of the local political economy that encourage the country's participation in the international cocaine industry.

Related to this is the revolutionary activity in Peru dominated by Sendero Luminoso and, to a lesser extent, by the Movimiento Revolucionario Tupac Amaru (MRTA). Although Sendero is by far the stronger, both groups are competing for influence in the Huallaga Valley, the hotbed of coca growth. Reports indicate that Sendero "may be planning to set up an independent state in the country's central jungle - the heartland of Peru's lucrative coca trade" (*Latin American Weekly Report* 1991). Coca production in the region is the rebel movement's principal source of funding; it is estimated that Sendero receives US$20 to US$30 million annually from its role in producing the narcotic (*El Comercio* 1990).

There appears to be a significant alliance between the coca growers and Sendero or the MRTA, ties which presumably have to do less with ideology and more with material necessity. The rebel groups strive to represent the interests of the growers, exemplified by Sendero's effort to obtain higher prices from Colombian traffickers for coca paste as well as to reduce the potential for intimidation of growers by traffickers. Furthermore, guerrilla groups oppose the U.S. proposal for aerial spraying of the Huallaga Valley with chemical defoliants such as Spike, and they also protest the use of biological defoliants.[4] In other words, the revolutionary groups protect the coca farmers from attempts by the Peruvian government and the United States to eradicate crop production. A major strategic problem for Lima and Washington is that the local population perceives that Peruvian and U.S. military forces work against their direct economic interests.

Militarization of the region has occurred at a breakneck speed. The U.S. Congress approved $125 million for military assistance to the Andean countries for 1989-90 (*Página Libre* 1990) and increased the 1991 total to $142.3 million (Institute of the Americas 1991). Former President Bush announced that these funds would also be used to combat leftist rebel movements in the region (*Página Libre* 1990).

It has been observed that the governments of the region, especially those of Peru and Bolivia, were reluctant to accept Washington's plans to militarize the situation. Nevertheless, "the 'stick' of legal sanctions and the 'carrot' of desperately needed foreign aid led President Fujimori to accept the military component in May 1991" (WOLA 1991).

Equally worrisome is that militarization of the problem is occurring against the backdrop of enormous human rights abuses. Amnesty International released a July 1990 report in Lima indicating that during the previous five years, Peru had the worst record of disappearances and illegal detentions on the planet (*Página Libre* 1990). Recent reports indicate that the human rights situation in Peru may be worsening (*Latin American Weekly Report* 1992). Thus, there is concern that the militarization of the drug problem exacerbates an already monstrous human rights situation.

Bolivia is caught in a similar, though less severe, situation than Peru. Economic impoverishment and the low global demand for legitimate exports, such as tin and coffee (Labrousse 1990; Craig 1987), have caused approximately three hundred thousand Bolivians to become involved in coca leaf production. Between eighty thousand and one hundred ten thousand hectares are cultivated for this purpose (Royal Canadian Mounted Police 1991), employing 20 percent of the adult work force (Andreas 1991-92; Gómez 1991). The country's US$600 billion in annual coca revenues in the early 1990s equaled the value of all its other exports combined.

Problems in Bolivia associated with coca leaf production and processing include increasing drug addiction among the local population, environmental degradation, corruption of local authorities, and massive regional disparities related to the influx of narco-dollars. Additional tension was created as a result of Washington's pressure on the Paz Zamora government to allow U.S. training of the Bolivian army. The agreement reached in April 1991 led to massive protests by labor groups, opposition parties, and the Catholic church, all of which threaten the stability of the country.

Colombia

As in the cases of Peru and Bolivia, the issues of narcotrafficking and narcoterrorism in Colombia need to be placed within the context of the country's political economy. It is useful to note at the outset that, while in the 1980s Latin America in general suffered its worst economic disaster since the Great Depression of the 1930s, Colombia's economy grew an average of 5 percent annually throughout the decade (Bagley 1990). This newly created wealth, nevertheless, has been skewed overwhelmingly toward the economic elite. In 1987, for example, business profits increased by 120 percent, while real salaries in the industrial sector decreased by 4 percent (WOLA 1989). Furthermore, Colombian government statistics reveal that 58 percent of the population lives in poverty (*Colombia Estadística* 1988, 2). America's Watch reports that the top 10 percent of Colombia's population receives 40 percent of the national income, while the bottom 20 percent subsists on only 5 percent (1986). In the countryside the top 3 percent of the landed elite own 70 percent of arable land, while 57 percent of regional farmers own 2.8 percent (WOLA 1989). This situation has been further exacerbated by the effects of narcoterrorism because peasants, unable to cope with the resulting terror, leave rural areas for what is typically an even less prosperous urban existence.

Despite the infusion of narco-dollars into the economy, the majority of the Colombian population remains poor. Against the backdrop of general impoverishment, approximately US$1 to $1.5 billion annually in cocaine profits was repatriated to Colombia in the late 1980s, representing approximately 3 percent of its yearly GNP (Tokatlián 1980; Chernick 1990). Most of the profit is made not in Latin America but by retailers in the North. The Medellín Cartel, Colombia's most prominent group of traffickers, has been listed in the *Fortune 500*, and Cartel leader Pablo Escobar has been reported as one of the world's wealthiest people.

While the Cartel's wealth apparently has provided narcotraffickers with significant political power, the Cartel has resorted to terrorism in an attempt to force the Colombian government to grant the legitimacy it desires (Araujo 1990). Political violence launched by narcotraffickers reached a crescendo in 1990 and early 1991. Tactics shifted from targeting socially prominent individuals opposed to drug trafficking to exerting terror on the public at large.

Superimposed upon the violent effects of narcoterrorism has been intense guerrilla warfare instigated by numerous competing leftist rebel groups. The alliance network in Colombia is significantly more complex than appears to be the case in Peru. For example, in some important areas narcotraffickers have experienced an ideological overlap with the Colombian State in that the cocaine cartels are fiercely committed to free enterprise and are vehemently anticommunist.[5] Ideologically, then, they find themselves aligned with a mainly pro-capitalist government (Pearce 1990).

The narcotraffickers also share an ideological alignment with the landed elite in the countryside who view the socialist guerrillas and their commitment toward a more equitable distribution of society's resources as their strategic and ideological enemy. Hence, the composition of, and support for, right-wing paramilitary groups has been rooted in the ideological alignment of narcotraffickers, the state, the landed elite, and moonlighting members of the police and army.

There are other complicating factors contributing to this shaky alliance. Refusing to accept the legitimacy of the narcotraffickers despite their ideological convergence has created a great distance between elements of the narcotraffickers, on the one hand, and the state and legitimate economic elites, on the other. Hence, violence emanating from narcoterrorists, from the guerrilla left, from the state in its war against both, and from criminal elements in Colombia reached extremely high levels in the late 1980s and early 1990s. Assassination represents the leading cause of death among males between the ages of 15 and 44 (Bagley 1990).

With regard to human rights, then, there exists a range of abuses in Colombia, those committed by guerrillas and narcoterrorists as well as by the state itself. The state's involvement in human rights abuses has been exemplified by military participation in illegal detentions, tortures, and massacres,[6] as well as aerial bombardments of villages suspected of sympathizing with the guerrilla left (Americas Watch 1989). In other cases, members of the armed forces participating in paramilitary groups engaged in violent human rights abuses are permitted to carry out their activities with the complicity of certain sectors of the government.

Colombia seemed to have reached its tolerance limit for violence by mid-1991. Attempts by traffickers to terrorize the population into accepting their legitimacy proved unsuccessful. Moreover, President César Gaviria's tough stance, combining a substantially bolstered military/police force with threats of U.S. extradition for traffickers if they did not surrender within a specified period, turned out to be effective. Leading cartel traffickers, such as Pablo Escobar, surrendered. Exhausted militarily by escalating government attacks, the majority of the guerrilla left also came to the bargaining table between 1990 and 1992 under an umbrella group called the Coordinadora Nacional Guerrillera Simón Bolívar (CNGSB). Both events were regarded as extremely positive and served to reduce the level of violence in the country.

The situation is, nevertheless, frail. The Cali Cartel is reported to have absorbed the market once controlled by the Medellín Cartel. Narcotrafficking in early 1992 is arguably as bad as ever, and there are reports that the country is now engaged in the cultivation of opium poppies and in the heroin processing trade (*Latin American Weekly Report* 1991). The spraying of defoliants in efforts to eradicate drug crop production has caused environmental protests throughout the country (*Latin American Weekly Report* 1992), and negotiations between the government and the CNGSB were stalemated at various points between late 1991 and early 1992. It is not clear how peace in Colombia will hold.

Canada and the Andean Drug War

While cocaine consumption patterns in Canada have risen over the last decade, as have increasingly large seizures of the drug, Ottawa's policy toward Latin America has also been affected by the cocaine epidemic in a number of significant ways. Canada concluded a $2 million program (1990-91) with the Colombian Departamento Administrativo de Seguridad (DAS) to assist Colombian security forces in the drug war by providing intelligence and surveillance equipment and bomb detectors (Maza 1990; Brown 1991; DEA 1992). The program has now been combined with an ongoing arrangement with the Royal Canadian Mounted Police (RCMP) to assist in training the security forces of Colombia, Peru, and other Andean countries. The RCMP also has representatives in Bogotá, Lima, and Caracas who specifically deal with the narcotics problem.

There exist a number of concerns and implications regarding the provision of Canadian security assistance to Colombia and Peru. A primary worry is that Canada's assistance to the Andean nations may be utilized for purposes beyond its intended goal of combating narcoterrorism. In that both Colombia and Peru have exceedingly poor records of human rights violations by the state and that both countries' governments are engaged in civil wars with leftist guerrillas, it is possible that well-intentioned Canadian aid might exacerbate the region's already horrendous human rights situation.

Canadian assistance, such as the provision of bomb detectors to Colombia, is obviously quite beneficial and contributes to the saving of lives rather than their destruction. Nevertheless, other types of assistance, such as Canada's training of security personnel and providing intelligence gathering equipment, may be used by Andean governments to combat the Left and/or indirectly support human rights abuses by the state.

While Canada's contribution is rather meager, it piggybacks the U.S. militarization of the region which amounted to US$142.3 million in fiscal year 1991. Thus, militarization of the problem is being spearheaded by the United States which has threatened to withhold other forms of assistance unless the regional governments cooperate with U.S. objectives.

Interest groups and concerned individuals have raised the issue of whether Canadian policy converged with Washington's apparent attempt to exert increased influence in Latin America (Bloomer 1991; Brown 1991). In this regard, *Semana,* a major Colombian news magazine (1990), criticized growing U.S. intervention in Colombia and the rest of Latin America and also suggested that Canada is working with the United States in a hegemonic project. Hence, the provision of Canadian security assistance to Andean countries has left Ottawa open to the charge that it supports U.S. efforts to increase its dominance in the region through military intervention.

This episode, then, raised the issue of the independence of Canadian policy in inter-American affairs. Elements of Ottawa's recent policy toward Latin America would tend to lend credence to the possibility that Canada's relations with the Andean countries were heavily influenced by U.S. interests. Canada, for example, was the only country in the Western Hemisphere, except El Salvador, to pronounce support for the 1989 U.S. invasion of Panama, a move that created a sour atmosphere for Canada's new position as a full member in the OAS. In addition to other policies, Ottawa's reinstatement, during the late 1980s, of developmental assistance to the staunch U.S.-client states of El Salvador and Guatemala as well as Canada's approach in the

Andean drug war were also interpreted by some as yet further evidence of an increasing convergence between the policies of Ottawa and Washington under the Mulroney government.[7]

Under criticism by Canadian interest groups and individuals as well as by Colombian journalists who charged that Ottawa supported U.S. interests in the region, Canada decided to terminate the US$2 million program. There were additional reasons behind this decision, not the least of which were severe fiscal constraints facing Ottawa. In addition, the Canadian government may have urged the termination of the project, since high-placed officials in the Latin American section of the Department of External Affairs (DEA) were generally critical of U.S. militarization of the Andean countries in fighting the drug war (DEA 1992). A clear evaluation of that program is required, examining whether it served Canadian interests or whether the policy contributed to the problem of militarization and conflict perpetuation. How Canada can assist in promoting conflict resolution and demilitarization in narcotrafficking and narcoterrorism in the Andean region is the central question. In this regard, there are definite linkages among conflict resolution, prospects for demilitarization, and developmental strategies.

Human rights abuses in Colombia have created a difficult climate for implementing aid programs. In an effort to reduce the chance of casualties among Canadian personnel, Ottawa now prefers to administer projects that train Colombians in Canada or that have Colombians perform fieldwork directed by a minimum number of Canadians.[8] A representative of a Canadian NGO working with the Colombian poor has suggested that as a consequence of the country's civil war, violence hindering NGOs' work in the countryside is primarily committed by the state or paramilitary groups. Regardless of the source of the violence, however, its presence has had a clear, negative impact on Canadian developmental assistance to Colombia.

In Peru, a "core country" recipient of Canadian assistance, the situation for aid delivery has deteriorated from a previously grim predicament. Canada's ambassador to the country indicated that project delivery has become a greater problem than in the past. In the likely event that it became necessary to pull out of the region quickly, the only projects that can be implemented are those that are short term (Charles 1990). DEA officials reported in 1992 that the situation had been further exacerbated by Sendero's guerrilla attacks on foreign aid workers.

Major questions emerge regarding how well existing developmental assistance policies address the social and economic roots fomenting drug production and trafficking as well as the consequences of conflict and militarization. Of particular importance is the Canadian effort to create income substitution programs able to reduce the propensity for coca growing in the region. Other existing programs, such as infrastructure creation, also require analysis in order to determine how effectively existing projects can be carried out within the context of the current civil war and militarization.

Another issue concerns the targeting of Canadians by narcoterrorists and others resentful of Ottawa's policy. As a result of the capture in New Brunswick of a plane flown by Colombians who were transporting cocaine during late 1989, narcotraffickers informed the Canadian Embassy in Bogotá they would retaliate against Canadians. Thus, innocent Canadians became victims of narcoterrorism.

Canadian commercial opportunities have also been negatively affected by narcoterrorism. The increasing unwillingness of businesspeople to travel to Colombia has contributed to sagging Canadian exports to the country. Exports have fallen to C$164 million in 1989 from C$224 million in 1987 (Brown 1991). Officials in Bogotá note that Canadian investment has dropped sharply due to the instability generated by narcoterrorism.

Similarly, Canadian exports to Peru have fallen from C$120 million in 1987 to C$56 million in 1989 (DEA 1990). Both narcoterrorism and Peru's drastic shortage of capital are responsible for this decline. While the larger picture suggests a further drop in Canadian commercial opportunities with Peru, a Canadian Government Fact Sheet lists Peru's defense requirements as a "main sector of interest for Canadian companies" (DEA 1990). Clearly, a multilateral solution to these severe problems needs to be constructed. Solutions must be sought through active cooperation of both drug-producing countries in the South and consumer nations in the North. One very useful venue for this approach is the OAS and, particularly, its Inter-American Drug Abuse Control Commission (CICAD). Canada became a member of CICAD in 1991 and should work within this agency to promote a multilateral solution to the narcotrafficking and narcoterrorism problems.

Formed in 1986, CICAD consists of the Latin American countries, Canada, and the United States. Its program is based on the following assumptions: 1) there is a relationship of socioeconomic development in the South with the phenomenon of narcoterrorism and trafficking; 2) policies must be pursued to reduce the market for and consumption of drugs; 3) global actions to combat narcotrafficking and terrorism must not impinge upon the sovereignty of producing countries; and 4) "...multilateral cooperation is becoming increasingly vital to the effectiveness of efforts to reduce the demand for drugs, prevent drug abuse, and combat unlawful trafficking in drugs" (OAS 1990). CICAD should be the central arena in which Canada formulates its domestic and global narcotics policies in concert with other key countries. Working within CICAD, Canada would follow its traditional position of seeking multilateral solutions to global crises and, thus, would be less susceptible to charges that it is working in collusion with Washington to achieve a broader U.S. agenda.

Canadian officials have identified some areas for improvement of CICAD. These include greater scrutiny for program proposals and their financial consequences as well as for addressing the issue of whether or not they duplicate other programs. Canada could also help improve the already excellent work performed by CICAD by creating a better evaluation process for existing projects (DEA 1992).

There exist at least six general issues that Canadian policymakers should consider within CICAD. The first is how Canada can work with other countries in the Americas to reduce drug consumption. This debate should focus on the amount of funding and attention that should be devoted toward drug interdiction, education, and eradication. Also pertinent is the issue of harmonizing national drug laws in the hemisphere.

Second is the question of which policies can be implemented in the short term to help alleviate the disastrous effects of narcoterrorism in the South. Raised here is the issue of whether Canada's provision of security assistance to Peru and Colombia should be continued in the future. Furthermore, it must be decided what kind of security assistance can be provided that combats narcoterrorism and trafficking but does not contribute to human rights violations. It also must be determined what type of assistance cannot be channeled toward civil warfare in the Andean region.

Third is a determination of the role Canada plays as a transit point for the flow of drugs to other locations. Related to this is the issue of Canada's role in drug interdiction. Current efforts by the RCMP in this regard should be explored and evaluated, and the role of the North

American Aerospace Defense Command (NORAD) in drug interdiction should also be probed.[9] Multilateral efforts at controlling the flow of narcotics will prove more effective than unilateral projects.

Fourth, additional attention should be devoted to Canada's role in the shipment to the South of vital chemicals for the production of drugs. Statistics indicate, for example, that Canada sold 1,334 kilograms of acetone to Colombia in 1989 (International Trade Division 1989). The extent to which Canadian exports of chemicals such as acetone, sulphuric acid, and kerosene are being utilized in drug production in South America must be examined, keeping careful watch on these transactions through CICAD.

The fifth issue concerns the extent to which Canada is involved in money-laundering activities and what can be done to prevent it. The Colombian DAS (1990) notes that narcotraffickers utilize Canada as a venue for money-laundering. However, the extent of this remains unclear, and this, too, requires further exploration from a multilateral perspective.

Sixth is the question regarding what types of aid policies can be formulated so that Canada promotes the long-term economic development of drug-producing countries. The executive secretary of CICAD suggests that long-term income substitution policies are crucial and that current crop substitution programs are short-sighted and ineffectual (Tragen 1990). Canada's ambassador to Peru suggests that other projects should also be explored (Charles 1990). Improving the commercialization and infrastructure for the shipment of local produce is just one example. Canada also has established programs to strengthen judicial agencies in Andean countries.

Coordinated inter-American assistance holds the most promise for successfully addressing the complex relationship between development and the drug war. Hemispheric trade, investment schemes, debt-packaging policies, and the establishment of reasonable prices for legitimate regional commodities are all issues that need to be analyzed multilaterally in an effort to promote development in the Andean region.

Conclusion

Canada has direct and varied interests in issues surrounding the hemispheric flow of cocaine and its role in the hemisphere's drug wars. These must be evaluated within the context of Canada's growing role in Latin American affairs. Since Canada is newly established as a major actor in inter-American relations, Ottawa's policies toward this crisis require the utmost consideration in order to avoid misadventures damaging to Canadian interests and influence in the region. Andean drug wars represent the most significant security problem in the hemisphere, and as an increasingly prominent player in the region, Canada must be active in devising policies to defuse the crisis.

It is clear that the U.S.-led militarization of the Andean region has not been successful in combating narcotrafficking, given the fact that "more cocaine is produced in more places than ever before" (Andreas 1991-2, 107). Thus, a different approach is required. Ottawa should engage in multilateral attempts at resolving the crisis in the Andes, particularly through CICAD. Finally, specific areas have been identified for additional Canadian research in order to better determine that country's contribution to the process of resolving the Andean drug crisis.

Notes

[1] For an excellent discussion of the empirical limits entailed in an analysis of narcotrafficking, see Ethan A. Nadelmann, 1990, "Latinoamérica: Economía Política del Comercio de Cocaína," in eds. Juan Tokatlián and Bruce Bagley, *Economía y Política del Narcotráfico* (Bogotá: Cerac), 31-56.

[2] As discussed in the OAS-sponsored conference, "Socio-Economic Studies for the Inter-American Specialized Conference on Drug Trafficking," in Rio de Janeiro, Brazil on August 22, 1986.

[3] For a broader discussion of the "safety valve" component, see José Hernando Gómez, 1991, "El Impacto del narcotráfico en el desarrollo de América Latina: Aspectos económicos," in José Hernando Gómez, *El Impacto de capital financiero del narcotráfico de América Latina* (La Paz, Bolivia: Centro para el estudio de las relaciones internacionales y el desarrollo).

[4] The United States continues to insist on the positive effects of Spike to eradicate coca production. A spokesperson at the U.S. military base in the Huallaga Valley indicated to me in an interview on July 19, 1990, that, "only radicals like Greenpeace" oppose Spike for environmental reasons. Environmental damage caused by Spike appears to be a real possibility. The Eli Lilly Company, a producer of Spike, in 1988 refused to accept any liability for damages to the people or ecology of the Huallaga Valley region if the defoliant were used. There have also been reports of U.S. biological weapons being used against coca production, see *Latin American Weekly Report*, 5 March 1992.

[5] The conservative viewpoint of narcotraffickers is well known, and there exists a plethora of literature on this point. A recent discussion appears in *Universal*, (Venezuela), 11 August 1990.

[6] The United Nations has issued reports linking the Colombian armed forces with assassinations of adversaries and with other human rights abuses. See *New York Times*, 3 March 1991.

[7] For an elaborated discussion of these and other elements of Canadian policy toward Latin America, see James Rochlin, 1990, "The Evolution of Canada as an Actor in Inter-American Affairs," *Millennium: Journal of International Studies* 19:2, 229-48.

[8] Interview with various officials at the Canadian Embassy, Bogotá, Colombia on July 31, 1990.

[9] For a cursory discussion of the role of NORAD in drug interdiction, see *Daily Courier* (Kelowna), 1990, 12 September.

References

Americas Watch. 1986. *The Central-Americanization of Colombia? Human Rights and the Peace Process.* Washington, D.C.: Americas Watch.

Americas Watch. 1989. *Informe sobre Derechos Humanos en Colombia.* Washington, D.C.: Americas Watch.

Andreas, P. 1991-92. "Dead-End Drug Wars." *Foreign Policy* 85 (Winter).

Appleton, Peter, with Doug Clark. 1990. *Billion $$$ High: The Drug Invasion of Canada.* Toronto: McGraw-Hill.

Araujo, Alfonso. 1990. "Páginas Internacionales." *El Tiempo.* July 24.

Bagley, Bruce. 1990. "Colombia y la guerra contra las drogas." In *Economía y política del narcotráfico,* eds. Juan Tokatlián and Bruce Bagley. Bogotá: CERAC.

Bloomer, Phillip. 1991. Director, Canadian University Service Organization. Interview. May 16.

Brown, Deane. 1991. Canadian Ambassador to Colombia. Interview. May 20.

Charles, Anne. 1990. Canadian Ambassador to Peru. Interview. July 13.

Chernick, Marc. 1990. "The Drug War." *NACLA Report on the Americas* (April).

Colombia Estadística. 1988:2. Bogotá, Colombia.

Craig, R. B. 1987. "Illicit Drug Traffic." *Journal of Interamerican Studies and World Affairs* 29 (Summer).

Daily Courier. 1990. September 12.

Department of External Affairs, Latin American Section. 1992. Interview with anonymous officials in Ottawa, Canada. March 13.

Department of External Affairs, Latin American Section. 1990. *Fact Sheet: Peru.* Ottawa: Department of External Affairs.

Departamento Administrativo de Seguridad (DAS). 1990. Press Release in Bogotá, Colombia. June 7.

Deustua, Alejandro. 1987. *El Narcotráfico y el interés nacional.* Lima: Centro Peruano de Estudios Internacionales (CEPEI).

Domestic Exports by Commodity and Country of Destination. 1989. Ottawa: Statistics Canada. International Trade Division.

El Comercio. 1990. July 28.

El Spectador. 1990. August 5.

Globe and Mail. 1990. September 12.

Gómez, José Hernando. 1991. "El impacto del narcotráfico en el desarrollo de América Latina: Aspectos económicos." In *El Impacto de Capital Financiero del Narcotráfico de América Latina.* La Paz: Centro para el estudio de relaciones internacionales y el desarrollo (CERID).

Institute of the Americas. 1991. *Seizing Opportunities: Report of the Inter-American Commission on Drug Policy.* San Diego: Institute of the Americas.

International Monetary Fund. 1986. *International Statistics.* Washington, D.C.: Johns Hopkins University Press.

International Trade Division, Statistics Canada. 1989. *Domestic Exports by Commodity and Country of Destination.* Ottawa: International Trade Division.

Labrousse, A. 1990. "Dependence on Drugs: Unemployment, Migration, and an Alternative Path." *International Labour Review* 129.

Latin American Weekly Report. 1991. January 24.

Latin American Weekly Report. 1991a. February 28.

Latin American Weekly Report. 1991b. December 5.

Latin American Weekly Report. 1992. February 27.

Latin American Weekly Report. 1992a. March 5.

Lee, R. 1990. "Tráfico de drogas y países en desarrollo." In *Economía y Política del Narcotráfico,* eds. Juan Tokatlián and Bruce Bagley. Bogotá: CERAC.

Maza, Miguel. 1990. General-DAS. Interview. July 25.

McClintock, Cynthia. 1988. "The War on Drugs: The Peruvian Case." *Journal of Interamerican Studies and World Affairs* 30 (Summer).

Nadelmann, Ethan A. 1990. "Latinoamérica: Economía política del comercio de cocaína." In *Economía y Política de Narcotráfico,* eds. Juan Tokatlián and Bruce Bagley. Bogotá: CERAC.

New York Times. 1991. March 3.

Organization of American States (OAS). 1990. *CICAD Information Document.* Comisión Interamericano Contra el Abuso de Drogas. May 23.

OAS-sponsored conference. 1986. "Socio-Economic Studies for the Inter-American Specialized Conference on Drug Traffic." In Rio de Janeiro, Brazil. August 22.

Página Libre. 1990. July 14.

Paredes, Carlos, and Jeffrey Sachs. 1990. *Estabilización y crecimiento en el Perú.* Lima: Brookings Institution.

Pearce, Jenny. 1990. "The People's War." *NACLA Report on the Americas* 23 (April).

Rochlin, James. 1990. "The Evolution of Canada as an Actor in Inter-American Affairs." *Millennium: Journal of International Studies* 19:2.

Royal Canadian Mounted Police (RCMP). 1991. *National Drug Intelligence Estimate - With Trend Indicators Through 1992.* Ottawa: Supply and Services.

Semana. 1990. "Showing Their Teeth: Concern in South America Regarding Increased U.S. Intervention." June 26.

Silva, Guillermo Rochaburn. 1988. "Crisis, Democracy, and the Left in Peru." *Latin American Perspectives.* Issue 58, 15:3.

Tokatlián, Juan. 1988. "National Security and Drugs: Their Impact on Colombian-U.S. Relations." *Journal of Interamerican Studies and World Affairs* 30 (Spring).

Tragen, Irving. 1990. Executive Secretary, CICAD, Organization of American States. Interview. September.

Tullis, F. LaMond. 1987. "Cocaine and Food: Likely Effects of the Burgeoning Transitional Industry on Food Production in Bolivia and Peru." In *Pursuing Food Security: Strategies and Obstacles in Africa, Asia, Latin America, and the Middle East (International Political Economy Yearbook,* vol. 3), eds. W. Ladd Hollist and F. LaMond Tullis. Boulder, Colo.: Lynne Rienner Publishers.

Universal. 1990. August 11.

Washington Office on Latin America. 1989. *Colombia Besieged: Political Violence and State Responsibility.* Washington, D.C.: WOLA.

Washington Office on Latin America. 1991. "Going to the Source: Results and Prospects for the War on Drugs in the Andes." June 7.

Chapter VII

CURRENT AND FUTURE DIRECTIONS FOR CANADIAN NGOS IN LATIN AMERICA[1]

Laura Macdonald

Introduction

Canadian non-governmental organizations (NGOs) have played an important role at the local level in Latin America in the areas of rural development and social infrastructure (such as providing education, health care, and sanitation). Despite the fact that NGOs are commonly perceived as apolitical, Canadian NGOs have also played a leading role in shaping official relations with Latin America. Without the public education and advocacy roles performed by certain NGOs, particularly over issues related to Central America, Canadian foreign policy might have been much more limited. Canadian NGOs have thus become important not just as vehicles of development assistance but also as links between civil societies in the North and South and as the nagging conscience of the Canadian state in its relations with Latin America. Recent changes in both Canada and Latin America have, however, called into question the traditional orientation of NGO activity and presented creative new opportunities for NGO action in cooperation with the Canadian state.

History and Evolution of Canadian NGOs

Canada has been a leader in recognizing the contributions NGOs make in the field of international development, and Canadian NGOs have in the past been pioneers in exploring new areas of NGO activity. As organizations of civil society,[2] they have mirrored the

---

Laura Macdonald is with Carleton University.

development of Canadian society as a whole. However, they have also been shaped by the expectations and policies of the Canadian state and the demands of their Third World partners.

Canadian NGOs have both influenced and benefited from the strain of what Cranford Pratt terms "humane internationalism" in Canadian public opinion: "Canada should do what it can to halt suffering, to relieve hardship, and to promote human welfare in countries beyond its borders and should deal equitably with them because it is right to do so" (1989, 24).

This ethical perspective is fragile and threatened, particularly in times of economic hardship, but does tend to differentiate Canadian attitudes from those of the United States. In the North-South Institute's study of Canadian NGOs, *Bridges of Hope?*, Tim Brodhead and Brent Herbert-Copley note that a 1987 U.S. public opinion poll found that only 54 percent of U.S. citizens favored providing any foreign aid at all; in contrast, a 1985 Decima poll revealed that 83 percent of Canadians supported existing levels of Canadian aid, while only 17 percent supported cuts in the aid budget (1988, 93n).[3]

Canadian humane internationalism, along with many Canadian NGOs, has religious roots. As elsewhere in the world, Canadian NGOs had their precursors in missionary societies (both Catholic and Protestant) but did not begin to take their current form until after World War II. The earliest groups, including Oxfam Canada, Canadian Save the Children Fund, CARE Canada, and Foster Parents Plan of Canada, were, in fact, established by foreign NGOs. Some of these groups subsequently became independent, and indigenous NGOs developed, but a significant number of Canadian NGOs, including some of the largest, are still responsible to foreign head offices. These NGO "branch plants" act primarily as fund-raisers, which is one reason that Canadian NGOs, in general, have fewer representatives in the field and less programming experience than U.S. NGOs (Herbert-Copley 1987).

Despite the largely foreign origins of the NGO phenomenon, the Canadian state was quick to recognize its potential. Canada was one of the first of the OECD nations to channel development assistance through NGOs on a responsive basis. In 1968, the newly established CIDA created an NGO division that disbursed C$5 million to twenty agencies in its first year. In part, the character of the NGO division reflected the Trudeau government's philosophical commitment to public participation in the foreign policy process. The Canadian government recognized that NGOs were best suited for local level community development work which was increasingly identified as the key to promoting self-reliance. NGOs also represent a primary source of information about Third World development for many Canadians, thereby creating a constituency for the government's aid budget. The Public Participation Program (PPP) was established within CIDA in 1971 to fund development education.[4] In contrast to large U.S. NGOs whose public outreach is largely limited to funding appeals, many Canadian NGOs (particularly those linked to the churches) view social change in Canada through education and advocacy as a fundamental part of their mandate.[5] In addition, a network of community-based learning centers has been established across the country and are largely dependent on PPP funds.

CIDA funding of NGOs expanded rapidly throughout the 1970s and 1980s as Canadian NGOs increased in number, size, and degree of professionalism. Total CIDA disbursements, adjusted for inflation, remained relatively stable through the 1980s, but the percentage channeled through the voluntary sector increased from 9 percent of the total budget in 1980-1981 to 18 percent in 1990-1991 (SECOR 1991, 49). Including private contributions, the international development work of Canadian NGOs in 1989-1990 amounted to over half a billion dollars (Smillie 1991, 8). NGO assistance thus represents some 20 percent of Canada's total aid effort.

The Canadian aid program has become increasingly complex in recent years. Tim Brodhead, former Executive Director of the Canadian Council on International Cooperation (CCIC), the umbrella group of Canadian development NGOs, states:

> One of the most dramatic changes in the last couple of years has been the move away from what was essentially a bipolar world when it came to development assistance in Canada: essentially, the bilateral or multilateral streams or, on the other hand, the non-governmental sector (Mills 1988, 14).

Several different "windows" for CIDA funding of NGOs have been created. The traditional mechanism for state funding of NGOs is responsive, with CIDA providing matching grants for projects or programs proposed by NGOs. Some multilateral assistance for disaster relief and refugee assistance is also channeled to NGOs through CIDA's

International Humanitarian Assistance division. Some NGOs feel that several recent trends in aid delivery threaten this traditional autonomy of setting their own priorities and retaining control over their use of funds. From the mid-1970s to the early 1980s with the establishment of the Country Focus Program, CIDA began to move toward increased use of non-responsive mechanisms. In this program CIDA established plans for bilateral assistance to a select number of recipient countries, contracting out part of the program to NGOs regarded as the best operators. While this made large amounts of bilateral aid funding available to some twenty of the larger, better-established NGOs, many feared loss of independence and increased vulnerability to the whims of government.[6]

Some NGOs feel that the decentralization of CIDA in the late 1980s has resulted in increased interference in their projects. While NGOs praise the intent of decentralization (greater CIDA contact with local realities and faster, more flexible responses), some criticize the effect on NGO activities and partnerships. Similar concerns have been expressed about the tendency for increased direct funding of Third World NGOs by CIDA, eliminating the Canadian NGOs as intermediaries. These changes in the government's relationship with NGOs signify that Canada is moving away from the European model of substantial autonomy for NGOs and closer to the U.S. model in which U.S. AID defines the parameters for aid delivery and then enlists NGO involvement.

In summary, Canadian NGOs have been distinguished in the past by rapid growth, a high level of state support, a growing autonomy from ties to international NGOs, and a significant commitment to development education and advocacy.

Profile of Canadian NGOs in Latin America

In contrast to the reluctance of the Canadian state until recently to make Latin America a priority of foreign policy, Canadian voluntary organizations have shown a strong interest in the region for decades. While as a region the Americas receive the lowest percentage of total Canadian overseas development assistance (ODA), they receive the highest percentage of ODA channeled through NGOs. This difference reflects the political priorities of NGOs as well as the strength of the voluntary sector in Latin America (see Table 1).

Table 1

Percentage of Total Canadian Overseas Development Assistance (ODA) by Region

Anglophone Africa	25%
Francophone Africa	22%
The Americas	15%
Asia	38%

Percentage of ODA through Voluntary Channels

Anglophone Africa	11%
Francophone Africa	7%
The Americas	24%
Asia	7%

Source: SECOR Group, 1991, *Strategic Management Review Working Document,* A study completed for the Canadian International Development Agency, October 9.

Canadian NGO involvement in Latin America has gone through four distinct phases. At first, missionaries from Quebec were particularly active in Latin America because of the strength of the Catholic religion in that province (McFarlane 1989). During this early phase, NGO aid took the form of charity. However, the radicalization of the Latin American church coupled with the gradual rejection of charitable forms of assistance among Canadian NGOs during the same period led to a second phase. In this subsequent period, NGOs shifted to support of grass roots development projects to promote local self-sufficiency.[7] Furthermore, the 1973 coup in Chile and the flow of refugees from the countries of the Southern Cone increased Canadian contacts with Latin Americans and pushed some Canadian NGOs to become more active in refugee assistance and human rights advocacy.

The 1979 Sandinista Revolution shifted attention to Central America and began a third phase in the 1980s which reflected a broader shift in Canada's view of the world — primarily toward Central America. While previous contacts between civil societies in the two parts of the hemisphere were limited and sporadic, the eruption of the Central American crisis brought Latin American concerns closer to Canadians in a new way. In particular, criticism of U.S. handling of that crisis led to calls for a more independent approach to Latin America, both at the state and NGO levels. Additionally, increased contact with the relatively strong and independent NGOs of Latin America influenced Canadian NGOs to redefine their joint relationships. As such, during the 1980s NGO involvement in Latin America expanded both quantitatively and qualitatively.

The Central American crisis of the 1980s profoundly challenged the common NGO claim of providing apolitical aid.[8] The politization of civil society in Central America meant that decisions to direct funds to certain countries or certain groups inevitably took on political connotations. This political dimension of NGO activity was much more controversial among U.S. NGOs. U.S. AID's greater influence over NGOs led to allegations that U.S. NGOs were tools of Washington's Central America low-intensity conflict strategy. Humanitarian assistance was seen as the carrot in the policy of gaining popular support for repressive regimes in El Salvador and Guatemala (Barry 1986). Similarly, the U.S. embargo on Sandinista Nicaragua meant that U.S. NGOs were unable to enlist government support for projects in that country. In contrast, European and Canadian NGOs became enthusiastic supporters of the new development model in that country, and they had their governments' financial support.

The Canadian government's perceived interests in Central America were much more limited, and the greater autonomy of Canadian NGOs meant that they were not perceived as a tool of government policy in the region. In fact, while many Canadian NGOs continued to perceive their work as apolitical, an increasing number became vocal participants in the public debate on Canadian foreign policy. At times this debate became quite heated. For example, Secretary of State for External Affairs, Joe Clark, was publicly criticized by representatives of Canadian NGOs in Nicaragua for not denouncing U.S. support of the Contras. The critique of Canadian policy in Central America also created dissension among NGOs when the Canadian Hunger Foundation (CHF) was chosen to administer a counterpart fund in El Salvador after Canadian bilateral assistance was resumed in 1984. In response, CCIC issued a statement opposing the resumption of Canadian official assistance to El Salvador, and CHF left the organization. However, the government also recognized the NGOs' expertise in the region, and it consulted with them in such forums as the House of Commons Sub-Committee on External Affairs and International Trade and the Special Committee on Central America. Policies promoted by NGOs included increased aid to Nicaragua, an elimination of official assistance to El Salvador and Guatemala, increased assistance to regional institutions, increased diplomatic representation in the region, and support for the peace process. NGOs' capacity to mobilize public opinion also gave them greater influence.

The intense interest of Canadian NGOs in Central America led to both formal and informal forms of cooperation among agencies. Those in El Salvador formed the El Salvador Monitoring Group to share information and denounce all forms of repression affecting the conduct of humanitarian work in that country. This later grew into the Central American Monitoring Group which lobbies the government on issues related to El Salvador and Guatemala. NGOs also attempted to expand and institutionalize their cooperation by creating a Central American Peace Fund. Formed by over eighty Canadian institutions, the Fund was conceived as a means of supporting the peace process in Central America through collaborative projects between Canadian NGOs and Central American partners. CIDA refused to meet the NGOs' demands for a three-to-one matching grant ratio, but the process of collective consultation on regional priorities encouraged cooperation and mutual understanding among those in the disparate NGO community.

A New Agenda for Canadian NGOs in Latin America

Recent changes are gradually creating the conditions for a fourth phase in Canadian NGO cooperation with Latin America. Although earlier approaches have completely disappeared, Canadian NGOs increasingly recognize the need to move away from a focus on specific communities (as in Phase II) and specific regions (Phase III) toward one of confronting issues of a hemispheric or global nature. These new issues imply a redefinition of NGOs' relations with their Latin American partners, since the Canadians confront the problems and potentiality of interdependence rather than being involved only as benefactors.

In part, the shift in NGO thinking is a defensive response to changes at home. Government budget cuts, perceived donor fatigue among the Canadian public, and organizational restructuring in CIDA seem to threaten the NGOs' funding base, or at least they seem to signal an end to the rather anarchical growth of the NGO sector that has occurred during the last two decades. These changes require NGOs to re-examine their operations critically, looking for ways to operate more efficiently, cooperate with each other, and devolve power to their

Third World partners. Ironically, then, despite these apparently negative trends, says CCIC, "There has probably never been a better time, nor a more urgent occasion, for change in the way Canadians and Canadian institutions organize themselves for the growing challenges of development" (1992, 7).

The danger, of course, is that financial pressures will cause NGOs to turn inward rather than seize new opportunities. Successive years of cuts and a "softening" of the aid budget to cover assistance to Eastern Europe or items not previously counted as aid have left NGOs feeling somewhat beleaguered.[9] Because NGOs like CUSO (Canadian University Service Overseas) received major cuts in last year's budget, they have had to undertake significant restructuring. Although CCIC does not have figures on the effects of the recession on private donations, there is a general impression that the existence of hundreds of NGOs, each with its own fund-raising campaign, is leading to "donor fatigue" among Canadians bombarded with financial appeals.

Compounding the uncertainty and instability arising from these financial pressures are concerns about the future direction to be taken by CIDA, particularly since a management review study recommended fundamental changes in the existing structure. The report, carried out by the SECOR Group, states that "CIDA is thoroughly buried under the weight of the aid delivery process and is in jeopardy of losing complete control over the development substance" (1991, 5). The report recommended a reduction in the number of countries served and a reconfiguration of CIDA's strategic system based on a "skills-driven approach," in which CIDA would improve its skills in policy research, strategic management, and analysis while executing agencies would play larger roles in the development and implementation of projects. However, no substantive study of the responsive program was undertaken, and the role to be played by NGOs remains unclear. CCIC is concerned that SECOR's proposal of a "more explicit and coherent policy focus," in which NGOs and other agents are contracted to implement CIDA-designed policies, "would be a dangerous step backward, closing off opportunities for innovation and the exploration of alternative strategies" (CCIC 1992, 3).

Changes occurring in Latin America also call for a fundamental re-examination of the raison-d'être of NGOs and how they operate. Despite the explosion of NGO assistance to Latin America over the last few decades, NGOs in both the North and South feel their work is undermined by macroeconomic conditions adversely affecting the poor, and they are, therefore, seeking ways of influencing policy debates at the national and international levels to represent the interests of those who otherwise lack a voice in these discussions.

The most important issues facing development efforts at the local level in Latin America in recent years are structural adjustment programs. Adopted by governments throughout the Third World, they have become a necessary condition for receiving IMF and World Bank approval. The restructuring of domestic economies has been promoted as a means of increasing Latin American countries' creditworthiness and competitiveness in order to enable them to take advantage of trade liberalization. Nevertheless, many NGOs argue that these programs have been undertaken without public consultation or concern for the social impact on the poor and that, in fact, the results have been increased levels of poverty and greater gaps between rich and poor. A recent report by the Inter-Church Fund for International Development and the Churches' Committee on International Affairs of the Canadian Council of Churches harshly criticized CIDA's linking of bilateral aid to Third World countries' acceptance of IMF and World Bank structural adjustment conditions (1991). While the churches share some of the international financial institutions' concerns about the inefficiency and corruption in many Third World countries that led to balance of payments problems, they criticize the following elements of CIDA's current strategy:

1. Canada's failure to emphasize the need for major reforms to the international economic system;

2. The erosion implicit in the IMF structural adjustment policies of the role of the governments of developing countries in legitimate regulatory, distributive, and national planning;

3. The full endorsement of a minimal-state, market-dominated, outward-oriented strategy as the formula for economic success in developing countries;

4. The frequent failure to shield the poor from the socially negative consequences of the policies insisted upon; and

5. The closer integration of CIDA's policies with those of the IMF and the World Bank (1991, 21).

Some have suggested, however, that NGOs can best use their energies in promoting "adjustment with a human face" — while accepting that some form of aid conditionality is inevitable. John Clark describes this approach:

> At the very least, this school argues that policy-based lending is here to stay and that it is rather more realistic to try to persuade the World Bank and others to modify their approach in favor of the poor rather than to relinquish conditionality. . . .The approach may sound paternalistic, but such a risk should be avoidable by ensuring that the new conditions are genuinely those articulated by the poor themselves through their people's organizations and NGOs (1991, 188).

In this view, NGOs, because of their experience with the effects of adjustment at the local level, are perfectly placed for dialogue with governments and international organizations about ways to reform adjustment programs to serve the needs of the poor effectively. NGOs can also play an important role by implementing grass roots development projects to ensure that the poor are able to survive some of the worst effects of structural adjustment and take advantage of some of its benefits, such as promoting the production of export crops by small and medium-sized peasant farms. Any of these responses to structural adjustment recognizes, however, that macroeconomic forces are the major determinant of the success of NGO work in the field. Canadian NGOs must adopt new methods of work and seek out new capabilities to respond adequately to this issue.

Just as NGOs have been forced to respond to structural adjustment, the growing number of free trade agreements being signed in the hemisphere will also impinge on NGO efforts in the coming years. Negotiations on NAFTA and EAI represent an important shift in hemispheric relations that has led to the direct involvement of some Canadian NGOs in political debates. The expansion of the CUSFTA to include Mexico has generated public debate on the issues of equitable socioeconomic development, international environmental standards, democratization and human rights, and equitable forms of North-South relations. As a result of their concerns about NAFTA, some Canadian NGOs are establishing links with Mexican NGOs. Seven development NGOs, in addition to several major churches, have joined Common Frontiers, a popular sector working group formed in response to the NAFTA talks.

Involvement in the NAFTA debate represents a new type of

political involvement for Canadian NGOs because the issues at stake affect Canadians as much as Mexicans. Thus, joint efforts with Mexican NGOs on this issue are based on shared interests rather than paternalism. According to one NGO representative, "the free trade issue underlines the point, once again, that it is no longer a question of 'us' and 'them.' On this one, we are all in it together" (Mably 1991). Through Common Frontiers, NGOs are also establishing closer relations with other elements of Canadian civil society, particularly the labor movement.

In addition, NGOs seem to have had some impact in shifting the terms of debate within Common Frontiers away from simple rejection of a trade agreement toward the type of development model Mexico should pursue. NGOs are raising concerns about how to achieve equitable, participatory, and sustainable development that responds to the needs of the majority of the population within the current context of globalization. Canadian NGOs working in Latin America may also be able to share their NAFTA experiences with their partners in the rest of the hemisphere.[10]

NGOs working in the area of the environment and sustainable development have always been aware of the pressing need to engage in lobbying and policy dialogue with governments and international organizations as well as in public education campaigns to achieve their goals. Indeed, their success in raising the issue of the environment as a development issue in the World Bank and elsewhere has made international organizations much more sensitive to the benefits of generally incorporating NGOs into the policy process. In recent years, environmental NGOs have expanded their emphasis on Third World concerns, while development NGOs have attempted to integrate concerns for sustainable development into their projects. Preparations for the UN Earth Summit held in Brazil during June 1992 (and the parallel NGO conference) brought to the fore the importance of addressing North-South issues.

Again, Canadian NGOs have an important role to play in representing Latin American concerns to the Canadian government as well as in the promotion of sustainable development projects at the local level. Additionally, there is potential for cross-fertilization between environmental and development NGOs. Environmental NGOs, which were born without the same access to state funds enjoyed by development NGOs, have always recognized the importance of lobbying and public education. Development NGOs, on the other hand, have an important role to play in insisting on the effective participation of Latin American communities in environmental programs and in ensuring that these communities' livelihoods are not sacrificed.

The processes of democratization that have swept the hemisphere in recent years are another area in which Canadian NGOs can play a vital role. Recent instability in Peru and Venezuela underlines the fragility of these processes. It is frequently suggested that in order to sustain democracy over the long term, institutions of civil society must be strengthened. One Chilean NGO representative thus stated in 1989, "The realization of national and local plans should not be the exclusive preserve of the state. NGOs can be efficacious channels for expression of civil society, enhancing popular participation at the local level."[11]

Since Latin American NGOs are almost entirely dependent upon foreign funding, support from Canadian NGOs can contribute to the strengthening of civil society and the process of democratization in Latin America. Little is understood, however, about the role played by NGOs in democratization and the types of programs and partnerships most likely to contribute to this role.[12]

The increasing capabilities and desire for independence on the part of their partners in the region is related to a final issue of democratization and is a fundamental point shaping the role of Canadian NGOs in Latin America. Many Latin American NGOs, now having several decades of existence and staffed by skilled and dedicated professionals, have come to resent constant intervention by Northern NGO funders. Thus, Latin NGOs are increasingly demanding that their relationships be established on the basis of true partnerships between equals rather than traditional paternalism, and they would require that Canadian NGOs move away from active involvement in the management of projects toward more strategic forms of support such as training and information sharing. Latin American partners also frequently state that Canadian NGOs can be most effective in reversing the processes of underdevelopment by engaging in policy debates and public education in Canada. Meeting the changing expectations of their partners, therefore, is the primary reason Canadian NGOs must find a new way of working if they are to justify their continued existence.

Canadian NGOs are not about to abandon their traditional roles in Latin America entirely. However, the issues outlined above make it increasingly clear that action at the local level alone is inadequate. Canadian NGOs must adapt to new roles in influencing policy both in

Canada and in Latin America — moving from the margins to the center of the development process. In order to achieve this transition, however, they must seriously address some of the weaknesses in their current organizational structures. Some of these weaknesses are associated with a tendency toward insularity which causes newcomers to find it difficult to break into the NGO world. Perhaps because of their dependence on government funding, Canadian NGOs have also tended to isolate themselves from other groups in Canadian society. In an era of increased competition for state funds, NGOs need to establish stronger ties and strengthen NGO links with universities and the private sector. Each of these sectors could inject new ideas and energies as well as provide political support for international development.

Research and policy development are other areas NGOs will need to develop if they wish to adapt to future challenges. A study by Ian Smillie, commissioned by CCIC, about new forms of cooperation between NGOs and CIDA states that the strongest message from a 1990 CCIC consultation between Canadian and Southern NGOs related to the weakness of the Canadian NGO analytical and research base. Smillie suggests that funds be established to support research on issues related to the development of voluntary sectors in Canada and the South (such as the informal sector, small-scale enterprise development, gender and the environment, the importance of NGOs in democratic pluralism, and management development) as well as to key areas of policy debate. Smillie also suggests that NGOs move beyond current ad hoc and informal forms of consultation with CIDA toward more regular forums where policy can be discussed "without acrimony and fear" (1991, 37).

In addition, NGOs will have to devote more attention to their own human resource development. NGO staff are frequently so overloaded with the day-to-day demands of project management that they lack time and institutional support for upgrading their skills. They are, thus, often poorly equipped to respond to the emerging areas of concern in the developing world. In particular, they lack skills in the areas of sustainable development, international political economy, and communications, which are crucial in the immediate future.

Finally, the relationship between NGOs and the Canadian government must be revised. As Smillie suggests, hostility and mistrust exist on both sides of the relationship, which are detrimental to effective communications. While some NGOs have distanced themselves from the policy process in order to maintain their supposed apolitical status, others assume that lobbying will be ineffective because of the dominance of CIDA by commercial interests or bureaucratic inertia. In addition, many NGOs fear that taking a political position will risk alienating both government and private funders, especially on controversial issues such as NAFTA. Meanwhile, CIDA officials tend to be overly defensive and insulate themselves from public criticism. The SECOR study of CIDA discusses the tendency of personnel to be overly cautious and highly resistant to change (1991, 11). NGOs are often seen as either extensions of government policy or unwelcome irritants to busy bureaucrats. Attitudes on both sides work against the exchange of information, analysis, and opinions which would enrich Canada's development effort.

Conclusion

Canadian NGO assistance to Latin America reflects the evolution of broader social, economic, and political forces in the hemisphere as well as Canadian and Latin American ideas about development cooperation. While this is a heterogeneous grouping with widely varying approaches, it is possible to discern a gradual evolution of Canadian NGO assistance in recent decades. The move away from charity and relief efforts toward small-scale development projects is aimed at local self-reliance. While NGOs have contributed much to development at this level, many factors are pushing them to play a different role in future Latin American development. Budgetary pressures at home will mean that Canadian NGOs will have to make better use of their resources. At the same time, increasing recognition of the weight of national and international forces in local development efforts are forcing them to focus their efforts more intensely on policy design and implementation, lobbying, and coalition formation. Such a strategy brings with it the risk of alienating government funders upon which Canadian NGOs are largely dependent. However, governments need to recognize the unique contributions NGOs have to make. NGOs' experience at the grass roots level and their capacity to establish linkages between civil societies in Canada and Latin America have the potential of generating development strategies that take into account the impact on the poor while simultaneously strengthening public support for Latin American development.

Notes

[1] Thanks to Tim Draimin and Katharine Pearson of CCIC for their helpful comments on an earlier draft.

[2] Note that while it is common for NGOs to identify themselves as part of civil society and thus essential for democratization, what constitutes civil society is seldom defined. See Macdonald 1992.

[3] Brodhead and Herbert-Copley (1988) suggest that this difference is partly the product of Canadian NGOs' greater focus on development education, relative to their U.S. counterparts.

[4] U.S. AID did not create a similar fund until 1981. While the Canadian PPP provides about C$6 million annually for development education, U.S. AID provides only US$1 million to its much larger NGO community (Smith 1984, 131). Larry Minear states that despite some increased interest in development education and advocacy in the U.S. NGO community, U.S. NGOs have not "been effective voices for an alternative approach to international development," nor have they moved beyond self-interested forms of advocacy (1987, 203).

[5] Nevertheless, the North-South Institute study showed that development education represented only 3 percent of respondents' budgets.

[6] The much-publicized problems of World University Services of Canada (WUSC) in 1990-91 are an example of the possible risks associated with excessive dependence on CIDA. WUSC, one of the main beneficiaries of CIDA contracts, saw its CIDA funding cut entirely and then reinstated on a more limited and highly controlled basis. The Country Focus Program is being phased out but may be replaced with another approach, "Integrated Country Programming," which was studied in the CIDA-contracted Strategic Management Review carried out by SECOR Inc. Consultants (Smillie 1991, 9).

[7] See the influential characterizations of NGO "generations" of activities by David Korten and the useful critique by Brian Murphy (Korten 1987 and 1990; Murphy 1991).

[8] This is largely a North American concern. European agencies are more likely to recognize the political significance of their work, and some even provide direct support to political parties of affiliated political alignments.

[9] The February 1991 budget announced a C$1600 million reduction in projected expenditure through to 1995-1996, amounting to a reduction of C$4 billion since 1988-1989 (Smillie 1991, 6).

[10] In a working paper by Paul Mably of OXFAM-Canada on the benefits of Canadian development and NGOs' participation in the Common Frontiers alliance, he notes three main ways in which free trade affects Canadian NGO work in the Americas: 1) effects in Latin America and the Caribbean - effects

of structural adjustment on living standards, environmental conditions, and wage levels; 2) effects on employment and sovereignty in Canada; and 3) the effect of rising levels of unemployment in Canada on NGOs' fund-raising base (Mably 1991).

[11] Francisco Vio of the Centro Canelo de Nos, quoted in Brian Loveman (1991, 11). The Loveman article also notes Vio's concern after the Aylwin government took power that it was continuing the statist tradition in Latin American societies and failing to incorporate popular participation adequately into the process of democratization.

[12] Support for civil society was one of the main criteria discussed by Canadian NGOs working in Central America during their attempts to establish a Peace Fund for the region (CCIC 1990). See also Macdonald 1992.

References

Barry, Tom. 1986. *Low-Intensity Conflict: The New Battlefield in Central America*. Albuquerque: Inter-Hemispheric Education Resource Centre.

Brodhead, Tim, and Brent Herbert-Copley. 1988. *Bridges of Hope? Canadian Voluntary Agencies and the Third World*. Ottawa: North-South Institute.

Brodhead, Tim. 1987. "NGOs: In one year, out the other?" *World Development*, 15: Supplement (Autumn).

Canadian Council on International Cooperation. 1990. "Canadian NGO Options in the Context of the Central American Peace Process." Ottawa: CCIC.

Canadian Council on International Cooperation. 1991. "Comments on the Secor Report." (December) Ottawa: CCIC.

Canadian Council on International Cooperation. 1992. "CCIC Response to the SECOR Report on CIDA's Strategic Management Review." (March) Ottawa: CCIC.

Carty, Robert. Unpublished. "Promises Unkept - CIDA: Four years after Winegard," #1 Costa Rica report for the Inter-Church Fund for International Development.

Clark, John. 1991. *Democratizing Development: The Role of Voluntary Organizations*. West Hartford, Conn.: Kumarian Press.

Fox, Thomas H. 1987. "NGOs from the United States." *World Development*, 15: Supplement (Autumn).

Herbert-Copley, Brent. 1987. "Canadian NGOs: Past Trends, Future Challenges," *World Development*, 15: Supplement (Autumn).

Inter-Church Fund for International Development and Churches' Committee on International Affairs, Canadian Council of Churches. 1991. *Diminishing Our Future - CIDA: Four Years After Winegard*. (October).

Korten, David C. 1987. "Third-Generation NGO Strategies: A Key to People-Centered Development." *World Development* 15: Supplement (Autumn).

Korten, David C. 1990. *Getting to the 21st Century: Voluntary Action and the Global Agenda*. West Hartford, Conn.: Kumarian Press.

Loveman, Brian. 1991. "NGOs and the Transition to Democracy in Chile," *Grassroots Development*, 15: 2.

Mably, Paul. 1991. "Free Trade Impacts on the Work of Canadian NGOs: The Need for NGO Action." (Unpublished paper presented in August 1991 in Ottawa).

Macdonald, Laura. 1992. *Supporting Civil Society: Non-Governmental Assistance to Costa Rica and Nicaragua*. Ph.D. Dissertation. North York, Ontario: York University. (January).

McFarlane, Peter. 1989. *Northern Shadows: Canadians and Central America*. Toronto: Between the Lines.

Mills, Don. Unpublished. "The Concept of Direct Funding and Implications for Caribbean Non-Governmental Organizations." Unpublished paper prepared for CUSO (June 1988).

Minear, Larry. 1987. "The Other Missions of NGOs: Education and Advocacy." *World Development* 15: Supplement (Autumn).

Murphy, Brian K. 1991. "Canadian NGOs and the Politics of Participation." In *Conflicts of Interest: Canada and the Third World,* eds. Jamie Swift and Brian Tomlinson. Toronto: Between the Lines.

Pratt, Cranford. 1989. "Canada: An Eroding and Limited Internationalism." In *Internationalism Under Strain: The North-South Policies of Canada, the Netherlands, Norway, and Sweden,* ed. Cranford Pratt. Toronto: University of Toronto Press.

SECOR Group. 1991. *Strategic Management Review Working Document.* A study completed for the Canadian International Development Agency. October 9.

Smillie, Ian. 1991. "A Time to Build Up: New Forms of Cooperation Between NGOs and CIDA." Study commissioned by the Canadian Council for International Cooperation. Ottawa (December).

Smith, Brian H. 1984. "U.S. and Canadian PVOs as Transnational Development Institutions." In *Private Voluntary Organizations as Agents of Development,* ed. Robert F. Gorman. Boulder, Colo.: Westview.

Chapter VIII

WRESTLING WITH HISTORY: PROSPECTS FOR PEACE IN ABORIGINAL-CANADA RELATIONS

Frances Abele

In all of the Americas and for several centuries, the long encounter of indigenous and exogenous (especially African and European) civilizations has been a cataclysm at the core of political and social development. This encounter has powerfully influenced the history, state structure, national myths, and political parameters of each nation-state.

For each country the character of the encounter varies considerably according to the nature of the original indigenous civilizations (gatherer-hunter, agrarian, democratic, tributary, sedentary, or nomadic), the nature of European progression (peaceful, warlike, in great numbers, or gradually), and with the colonizers' aspirations to establish a slave-based mode of production, a Christian dominion, peaceful coexistence, or a busy trading relationship, among others.

Whatever the initial terms, and whether the foreign emissaries sought gold, spices, fur, fish, or timber on behalf of Spain, Portugal, France, or Great Britain, the visitors tended to have an early, devastating effect on the indigenous populations they encountered. Military matters aside, the exchange of fatal diseases damaged the Americas

This essay was begun when I was Associate Professor of Public Administration, Carleton University, Ottawa, Canada, and it was finally completed during my secondment to the research directorate of the Royal Commission on Aboriginal Peoples. I am grateful to my colleagues at Carleton University, the participants in a seminar at the North-South Center at the University of Miami, and especially to Edgar J. Dosman, for stimulating consideration of these ideas. I am indebted, as usual, to the kind personal support and intellectual companionship of my husband, George Kinloch. None of the people to whom I am grateful, nor the Royal Commission, should be blamed for or associated with my analysis.

131

with the result that indigenous civilizations were severely weakened and sometimes even literally decimated or annihilated by the common infections of Europeans and Africans.[1]

If all countries of the Americas have the original encounter of the multiple civilizations of the Western and Eastern Hemispheres in common, we all also share the uneven and often tragic legacy and, I believe, the understandable tendency to mythologize or deny the frequently genocidal consequences. To my knowledge, no American country has resolved peacefully and finally the issues of ethnic and national blending and accommodation. There are, though, very great differences in kind and in degree of problems, particularly the role of violence and the extent to which skin color and nationality are associated with privilege and disadvantage.

This paper explores the dimensions of this hemispheric process in one American country, Canada. After reviewing some basic facts about Canada, it reviews recent history to create a context for pondering the significance of the standoff between Mohawks and the Canadian Armed Forces in the hot summer of 1990 and the limited success enjoyed by aboriginal peoples in Canada's most recent (1992) constitutional embroglio.[2] These two events, apparently paradoxical, are, in fact, intimately related polar dimensions of the same changing relationship. Finally, the paper lists and briefly discusses the other features of Canada's attempt to wrestle with history and to find a means of peaceful coexistence.

Background

Self-identified indigenous people comprise between 3 and 5 percent of Canada's population. Of the remainder, about one-third are Francophone and two-thirds are Anglophone, but in terms of ethnic origin both language groups are extremely heterogeneous. Leaving Viking settlements aside, sustained contact between Europeans and aboriginals in what is now Canada began in the East with the arrival of exploring traders and fishers in the sixteenth century and in the West (involving Russians) about one hundred years later. Canadians tend to believe that, especially in the latter contact period, frontier relations were more peaceful than they were in the United States and in many parts of Central and South America. This is only somewhat true. There were sometimes murders of the earliest peoples encountered, and over the contact period there were some violent but isolated skirmishes involving relatively small numbers of people. The military maneuvers sometimes still called "The French and Indian Wars" involved aboriginal peoples living on either side of the border between the present countries of Canada and the United States. In what is now Canada there was one major insurrection of the prairie Metis and their allies. On the whole, however, the colonization of Canada and the displacement of aboriginal peoples were both quite orderly, if order can be considered to include the ravages of contagious diseases that annihilated entire populations. However, there were no sustained Indian wars and no great relocations of First Nations such as occurred in the United States. Part of the reason for this lies in the fur trading practices of the early French colonists and part in that most treaties were negotiated with the Crown, not with locally mandated entrepreneurs, a circumstance that lent somewhat more order and predictability. In general, attempts to abolish and assimilate the First Nations followed the long depredations of disease and the entrenchment of Christian religions and were administratively coercive, rather than military.

Canada was established as a British colony, and *as a colony* evolved slowly toward sovereign status. Some important benchmarks are 1867 (federation of four eastern colonies), 1931 (establishment of a foreign policy authority independent of Great Britain), and 1982 (patriation of the constitution, which meant, in part, transfer to Canada of the right to amend the constitution).[3] However, there was no revolutionary moment, no single founding event or agreement, and no assertion of citizen rights, individual or otherwise. From the beginning, the Canadian constitution has been a work-in-progress, and it is, of course, still incomplete. There have been many more failed attempts at constitutional change than there have been successes.

Yet the basic terms of the federation are not in doubt. Canada is a parliamentary democracy based on the Westminster model with the important modifications that 1) it is a federal, not a unitary state, including ten provinces and two territories forming the subnational jurisdictions; 2) from the beginning, the constitution has recognized special collective rights for Francophones; and 3) as opposed to the case in Great Britain, Canada has had since 1982 a written constitution that incorporates a somewhat conditional Charter of Rights. (The Charter of Rights is conditional in the sense that its effect on individual rights is moderated by acknowledgment of collective rights of

Francophones in Quebec.) Thus, Canada has an inherited, not consciously designed, state structure revised by its citizens from a model which had evolved over centuries in a unitary kingdom that became the center of a great empire. In Canada, this form of governance was adapted to incorporate "two nations" (of French- and English-speaking settlers) and geography (which in the late nineteenth century virtually dictated some sort of federalism).

The British heritage, geography, and the proximity of a dynamic industrial and military power, the United States, from the beginning have predisposed Canadian politicians to use the state unselfconsciously for economic purposes. This, in turn, has created the possibility of a social democratic social welfare system. Given all this, it is probably not surprising that increasingly but fractiously revising the terms of the federation is a persistent Canadian preoccupation. In October 1992 Canada concluded a particularly difficult round of constitutional negotiations. This round included an impressive range of political processes, including elite accommodation, the traditional Canadian resort to task forces and studies, and extensive citizen participation (which stopped short, however, of the use of a constituent assembly to develop a new constitutional agreement). In much of this discussion, the central issue was the extent to which and the means by which the self-defined collectivities of Francophones in Quebec and aboriginal peoples throughout Canada could flourish in the future. The constitutional discussion began as a process to include Quebec in the national consensus, since this province opted out of the 1982 patriation and ratification process; as the struggles have unfolded over the last decade or so, aboriginal peoples have been successful in counting themselves in.[4]

The Politics of Constitutions and Extra-Parliamentary Action

The following sequence of events illustrates important features of the evolving relations between aboriginal peoples and Canada in recent years:

- Native political activism was discouraged and often repressed vigorously until about thirty years ago, while state policies toward aboriginal peoples were more or less frankly assimilationist. This position was reflected in the policy that denied the franchise to those who were "registered" Indians.[5] The year registered Indians were permitted to vote in federal elections, 1960, makes a convenient end-marker for this period (Berger 1981; Kulchyski 1988).

- The three decades after 1960 saw an enormous process of community organizing, mobilization, internal debate about strategy, constitutional and governance matters, and development of solidarity networks as aboriginal peoples sought the means to explain and promote their political goals. In this period there were many disappointing reversals, as well as victories, and long periods of confusion (Cardinal 1979; Dosman 1972; Boldt and Long 1985). Relations between aboriginal peoples and the rest of Canada, as well as relations within aboriginal communities and nations, were dramatically transformed.

- Aboriginal peoples' political mobilization also produced reasonable levels of federal funding, both for general institutional support of advocacy and representative organizations. A tradition of federal funding for special projects — such as research on key policy questions — was established. A dense network of linked political organizations at the community, regional, tribal, and federal level, a semi-autonomous network of aboriginal women's organizations, and another network of special services organizations (in policing, child welfare, communications, and health, among others) evolved rapidly.

- The culmination of much of the work in "high politics" of the 1970s was the project to have aboriginal and treaty rights entrenched in the soon-to-be patriated Canadian constitution.[6] This project was successful in 1982 when "existing aboriginal and treaty rights" were entrenched, as was a process through which the prime minister and provincial premiers were to reach agreement with the representatives of aboriginal peoples about what that phrase meant. The process called for a series of First Ministers' Conferences (FMCs) on Aboriginal Matters.

- In May 1987 the last FMC ended with virtually no progress having been made since 1982. In the end, the premiers and prime minister were unable to agree about legal and fiscal matters.

- Just one month later, in June 1987, another, less public process culminated in an agreement among the same provincial premiers and prime minister. They were able to reach an agreement to recognize Quebec as a distinct society — among other provisions — in what came to be known as the Meech Lake Accord. The Accord among the leaders of the federal and provincial governments was presented to the Canadian public, with a three-year timetable for discussion and ultimate endorsement by the provincial and federal legislatures. The Meech Lake Accord, whatever its other virtues, ignored aboriginal peoples' aspirations.

• After 1987, the federal Cabinet neglected to replace the lapsed first ministers' process with any other measures to address outstanding aboriginal governance issues systematically.

• In June 1990 Elijah Harper, an aboriginal member of the Manitoba legislature, acted with the support of many Canadians and all aboriginal organizations to block endorsement of the Meech Lake Accord by taking advantage of a legislative technicality. On the heels of this event — although certainly not in direct response to it — the Quebec provincial police force, the Sûreté du Québec, mounted an armed attack, which failed, on Mohawk barricades at Oka, Quebec. Such barricades and other forms of peaceful civil disobedience are a common resort of aboriginal peoples in Canada since they lack the numbers and financial resources to press their cause in other ways. In the Oka case the barricades were a last-ditch effort to prevent expansion of a municipal golf course onto what might generously be described as "disputed" territory (York and Pindera 1992; Horn 1991).

• The June 1990 confrontation at Oka was unusual in at least two respects. Some of the Mohawks who were eventually drawn into the process were armed, and the Canadian Armed Forces (CAF) were directed to intervene after the Sûreté bungled the enterprise. Canadians were, in general, shocked. While civil disobedience is a reasonably common political tool of aboriginal people in Canada, protestors rarely resort to arms or physical coercion of any kind. Similarly, the bread and butter domestic assignment of the Canadian military is search and rescue; Oka was only the second time in over fifty years that the CAF had been used for domestic peacekeeping.[7] The confrontation at Oka ended peacefully after a tense ninety-day siege, but not before there were a number of nationally televised racial confrontations in Quebec, demonstrations of support for the Mohawks by natives and non-natives all over Canada, and another instance of armed civil disobedience in Alberta.

- After about a year of disarray following the 1990 collapse of the Meech Lake Accord and the confrontation at Oka, the federal Cabinet produced a new process for reaching constitutional consensus. Where the earlier process had consisted of largely secret elite negotiations, the second involved several special commissions, parliamentary committees, and public consultative processes.

- The culmination of the new process of consultation and public deliberation was a national plebiscite on what became known as the Charlottetown Accord. This agreement, like the Meech Lake Accord, was the product of secret elite negotiation, but there were significant differences from the earlier Meech Lake process. This time, elites negotiated on the basis of a wide public discussion of concrete proposals from a number of sources, including the federal Cabinet. The scope of elite representation was also expanded to include territorial as well as provincial leaders, and — for part of the process — the aboriginal leadership as well.[8]

- The plebiscite asked Canadian voters to endorse or to reject the Charlottetown Accord, which in many respects followed the broad outlines of the 1987 Meech Lake Accord. There was at least one major difference, however: the Charlottetown Accord acknowledged the "inherent right to self-government" of aboriginal peoples in Canada. The Charlottetown Accord was rejected by a majority of voters, but apparently not, in most parts of the country, because there was resistance to the inherent right to aboriginal self-government.

In the preceding story about what has been happening in the "high politics" of aboriginal affairs in Canada over the last thirty-odd years, there are a number of interesting features — for example, the ways in which Quebec and First Nations have blocked each others' constitutional progress to date — that cannot for reasons of space be pursued here. Suffice it to say that emerging from all the recent convulsions is growing acceptance in Canada (and in the Conservative federal cabinet) that any new constitutional amendments will recognize aboriginal peoples' inherent right to self-government. The inherent right has long been the "bottom line" of aboriginal negotiators; the consensus among the Canadian political elite to constitutionally affirm this right marks a major change in aboriginal-Canada relations. While further constitutional deliberations are likely to be deferred for a few years, at least until after the imminent federal and Quebec elections, it is difficult to imagine a permanent reversal of the acceptance by political elites of the principle.

During the past thirty years, aboriginal peoples have eroded paternalistic attitudes and shattered colonial administrations. They have developed an alternative set of institutions with substantial policy and service delivery capacity. Throughout the last ten years, they sought and nearly achieved full constitutional entrenchment of their own view of their relationship to the rest of Canada, effectively contradicting the vision that had informed federal policy since the formation of Canada. In the process they have opened a series of channels through which Canada's resolution of the dilemmas of the long intercontinental encounter of civilizations is being resolved. The following lists these and comments about their general significance.

Underlying Issues, Various Channels, and Interesting Solutions

Constitutional Entrenchment

Canadians will enjoy a much-needed respite from constitutional deliberations for at least three years while elections are held federally and in the pivotal province of Quebec. The issue of constitutional reform will undoubtedly reappear, to dominate the Canadian political agenda again, before the end of the decade. The debate will likely follow traditional lines, though there will probably be more carefully organized citizen participation and the involvement of aboriginal peoples from the beginning.

The Canadian political philosopher Charles Taylor has pointed out that in Quebec there is strong support for recognition insuring the survival of "the collectivity" as a community within which individuals may thrive. Collectivity rights are seen as complementary, not contra-dictory, to individual rights.[9] The rest of Canada more or less adheres to the classical liberal view of "the good regime" as one which is based upon individual rights, responsibilities, and freedoms. The two views on collective rights are frequently in conflict in Canada. Yet the Canadian constitutional compromise has always somehow satisfied both. Any changes in the future will likely share this characteristic of the earlier resolutions in that it will accommodate both visions in language sufficiently obscure to win the support of both linguistic communities. Aboriginal peoples, it now appears, are well advanced in the project of situating a similarly general form of constitutional "representation." That is probably as much as can be expected from the constitutional process, and it leaves much work to be done on other fronts.

Royal Commissions

Commissions of inquiry, often called Royal Commissions, are a tried-and-true means of defusing debate and diffusing dissent as well as of genuinely seeking solutions in Canada. There has been a series of Royal Commissions on aboriginal matters as well as a number of federal or provincial task forces with somewhat more circumscribed mandates. Currently, a federal Royal Commission of Inquiry on Aboriginal Peoples is in progress, and it has a very wide mandate for advising the government on all matters of aboriginal affairs. Four of seven commissioners are aboriginals, and the Commission is chaired jointly by an aboriginal leader (Georges Erasmus) and a Quebec judge (Rene Dussault). Although aboriginal peoples' experiences with Royal Commissions have not been uniformly happy,[10] hopes are high that this Commission will further educate the public, sustain the political attention of aboriginal citizens, and conduct research that will lead to concrete solutions to outstanding issues.

Negotiated Self-Government and Program Development

The political convulsions of the last thirty years have produced a number of processes through which aboriginal bands, and sometimes regional and tribal organizations, have won "devolution" of various administrative responsibilities. A simultaneous, complementary process has entailed development of a much larger, but still small, cohort of trained aboriginal bureaucrats and professionals (accountants, social workers, teachers, nurses, and many others) in organizational settings adapted to the aboriginal communities they serve. There is also a generic "self-government" negotiation process appealing to some First Nations, which involves negotiation of a comprehensive self-government agreement transferring (basically municipal) governing powers and resources to the aboriginal government. This form of self-government, protected in federal legislation but not in the Constitution, is seen as inadequate by many aboriginal people. However, those bands that have chosen this route see negotiated self-government as a step in the right direction, creating authentic self-government by stages.[11]

Comprehensive Claims Negotiations

Over half of Canada's land mass is not covered by treaty; sovereignty is thus contested in the territorial North, Labrador, and British Columbia. There is considerable jurisprudence which, over time, on the whole, has become more favorable to the aboriginal side. The federal response has been to negotiate "comprehensive claims," or modern treaties, with the indigenous inhabitants of the contested areas. Such claims have required long negotiations, but three agreements have been signed, and another is nearing completion.[12] The claims agreements involve a land settlement apportioning some territory to the aboriginal group and most to the Crown. Fairly large cash settlements, typically payable over twenty years, are made as compensation for lost revenue and title. In addition, in each successive claim, there are increasingly innovative provisions for shared management of resources, social planning functions, and in the case of the Inuit (Eskimo) claim on the eastern Northwest Territories, a provision to create a new, but still racially diverse and publicly governed territory in which the Inuit would form the majority. The earliest comprehensive claims agreements are somewhat similar to the Alaska Native Claims Settlement Act. However, the Canadian groups have tried to learn from the Alaskan experience, and they have taken advantage of the long duration of the process and the Canadian governing practices mentioned earlier to improve the terms. The case of Nunavut, a new territory that might be created along with settlement of the Inuit comprehensive claim, is particularly spectacular, especially in light of Canada's mixed experience with Quebec.

Internal Development

The four processes just reviewed share the characteristic of being primarily "other-directed," explicitly focused on or powerfully shaped by the relationship between aboriginal peoples and Canadian political institutions. Increasingly, aboriginal people are turning their attention to matters of internal development. The projects here are various. Aboriginal

women have formed organizations to address issues of gender representation — and political issues of particular salience to aboriginal women
— both within and against existing and future aboriginal governments.
The rising of women has occurred within communities and in the more
public forums of national political life. Many former male and female
politicians active at local and national levels are turning away from
political participation and toward matters of community economic
development and the formation of intra-community, regional, and
Canada-wide economic networks. Their attention is on community
healing and the promotion of individual and community prosperity.

These two developments have had important consequences for
the aboriginal political movement. Both tend to highlight the diversity
among aboriginal nations, and thus they put pressure on the "common
front" necessary for constitutional negotiations and high politics.
Conversely, they also strengthen the whole by advancing the project
of decolonization beyond reaction to and rejection of state domination
and toward the implementation of independence that creates the
possibility of peaceful cohabitation.

Conclusion

In 1930 Harold Innis, the first Canadian scholar to interpret Canadian
history as the confrontation of two civilizations (the indigenous and the
European), concluded his long study with the comment: "the 'lords of the
lakes and forest' have passed away," never again to be influential in
Canadian political, economic, and social development (Innis 1956).
Indeed, this view has been a persistent theme in much mainstream
Canadian scholarly writing, if the First Nations are mentioned at all. As the
introduction to this paper suggests, I think Innis' historical premise was
correct, even if his judgment about aboriginal decline was inaccurate.
Confronting the reality of existing aboriginal governments and societies
is central to understanding much of the history and current complexion
of events in our hemisphere — though it surely is not the only key.
Colonization of the Americas by people (and peoples) from every
continent of the world has created an American character that is, in
essence, heterogeneous, a potpourri of traditions, histories, preconcep-
tions, ruling values, and priorities. My attention has been on what is peculiarly
Canadian about the confrontation of civilizations in this context, even though
that is no more than a prologue to a discussion of common ends.

Notes

[1] Of hundreds of good general treatments, I like Bruce Trigger, 1976, *Natives and Newcomers* (Montreal and Kingston: McGill-Queen's University Press); Francis Jennings, 1988, *Empire of Fortune: Crowns, Colonies and Tribes in the Seven Years' War in America* (New York: W. W. Norton and Co.); Roy Harvey Pearce, 1965, *Savagism and Civilization* (Baltimore and London: Johns Hopkins Press); Robin Blackburn, 1988, *The Overthrow of Colonial Slavery 1776-1848* (London: Verso); and Eric R. Wolfe, 1982, *Europe and the People Without History* (Berkeley: University of California Press).

[2] I use the terms aboriginal peoples, First Nations, indigenous peoples, and natives interchangeably and eclectically in this paper, to refer collectively to those who are descended from the original nations of South, Central, and North America who were here when Europeans settled.

[3] The oversimplification becomes almost grotesque at this point, since I omit from consideration relations between early French settlers and the First Nations, the conquest of French Canada by the British, and the whole story of British colonial policy toward these transplanted Europeans and its ultimate realization in the Canada constitution. For Québecois, an equally important date is 1759, marking the conquest of French Québec by British forces.

[4] I am disregarding the efforts by other forces, such as the women's movement, to constitutionalize their progress toward equal treatment, and the important regionalist dimension to Canadian constitutional struggles. These are important matters, but there is not space to treat them here.

[5] Registration meant that an individual was listed by the federal government as being an Indian and entitled to the privileges that followed from that legal condition. These largely included receipt of benefits to which they were entitled as descendants of the signatories of treaties. In order to have the right to vote, and to exercise certain other citizen rights, registered Indians were required to renounce their status. In doing so, they became citizens like any others and no longer entitled to their treaty rights.

[6] For an exploration of the multiple dimensions of this project, and some implications, see David C. Hawkes, ed., 1989, *Aboriginal Peoples and Government Responsibility: Exploring Federal and Provincial Roles* (Ottawa: Carleton University Press), particularly the chapter by Frances Abele and Katherine Graham, "High Politics is Not Enough: Policies and Programs for Aboriginal Peoples in Alberta and Ontario."

[7] The other occasion was in 1970 when the cabinet apparently feared a violent separatist uprising in Quebec.

[8] In all previous constitutional negotiations, territorial leaders and leaders of aboriginal organizations had been "at the table" as observers, or not included at all. The inclusion of territorial leaders was an important advantage

for the aboriginal cause, since both territories contain a large proportion of aboriginal people, and both had governments particularly committed to advancing aboriginal interests.

9 The United States scholar Frances Svensson has made the case for collective rights as an essential aspect of individual rights. Frances Svensson, 1977, "Liberal Democracy and Group Rights: The Legacy of Individualism and its Impact on American Indian Tribes" *Political Studies* 27:3.

10 The unfortunate story of another Royal Commission is told in Sally Weaver, 1975, *Making Canadian Indian Policy: The Hidden Agenda 1968-1970* (Toronto: University of Toronto Press).

11 A full review of existing Indian governments is Frank Cassidy and Richard Bish, 1989, *Indian Governments in Canada* (Montreal: Institute for Research in Public Policy).

12 The first modern treaty was the James Bay and Northern Quebec agreement; the second was signed by the Inuvialuit of the Mackenzie Delta - Beaufort Sea area and the federal government in 1984. Somewhat different agreements have been nearly completed by the Council for Yukon Indians and the Tungavik Federation of Nunavut. Others are in progress, and, in addition, there is a waiting list of perhaps twenty more.

References

Berger, Thomas R. 1981. *Fragile Freedoms: Human Rights and Dissent in Canada.* Toronto: Clark Irwin.

Blackburn, Robin. 1988. *The Overthrow of Colonial Slavery 1776-1848.* London: Verso.

Boldt, Henno, and J. Anthony Long. 1985. *The Quest for Justice: Aboriginal Peoples and Aboriginal Rights.* Toronto: University of Toronto Press.

Cardinal, Harold. 1979. *The Rebirth of Canada's Indians.* Edmonton: Hurtig Publishers.

Cassidy, Frank, and Richard Bish. 1989. *Indian Governments in Canada.* Montreal: Institute for Research in Public Policy.

Dosman, Edgar J. 1972. *Indians: The Urban Dilemma.* Toronto: McClelland and Stewart.

Hawkes, David C., ed. 1989. *Aboriginal Peoples and Government Responsibility: Exploring Federal and Provincial Roles.* Ottawa: Carleton University Press.

Horn, Kahn-Tineta. 1991. "Beyond Oka: Dimensions of Mohawk Sovereignty." *Studies in Political Economy* 35 (Summer).

Innis, Harold. [1930] 1956. *The Fur Trade in Canada: An Introduction to Canadian Economic History.* Toronto: University of Toronto Press.

Jennings, Francis. 1988. *Empire of Fortune: Crowns, Colonies and Tribes in the Seven Years' War in America.* New York: W.W. Norton and Co.

Kulchyski, Peter. 1988. "A Considerable Unrest: F.O. Loft and the League of Indians." *Native Studies Review* 4: 1&2.

Pearce, Roy Harvey. [1953] 1965. *Savagism and Civilization.* Baltimore and London: Johns Hopkins University Press.

Svensson, Frances. 1977. "Liberal Democracy and Group Rights: The Legacy of Individualism and its Impact on American Indian Tribes." *Political Studies* 27:3.

Trigger, Bruce. 1976. *Natives and Newcomers.* Montreal and Kingston: McGill-Queen's University Press.

Weaver, Sally. 1975. *Making Canadian Indian Policy: The Hidden Agenda, 1968-70.* Toronto: University of Toronto Press.

Wolfe, Eric R. 1982. *Europe and the People Without History.* Berkeley: University of California Press.

York, Geoffrey, and Loreen Pindera. 1992. *The People of the Pines.* Toronto: Little, Brown.

Chapter IX

SECURITY ISSUES IN THE WESTERN HEMISPHERE OF THE 1990S: A CANADIAN PERSPECTIVE

Hal P. Klepak

A ny analysis of the security issues the Western Hemisphere will face over the remaining years of this decade poses more than its fair share of difficulties. The most obvious is judging the future, the most challenging of human desires and drives. The second is the complexity of the topic, as security in this hemisphere has always been multi-faceted and full of nuance. It has generally been seen in different ways in different capitals and times and by different social classes. Third, there is the problem of trying to give a Canadian perspective to issues which, to date, have been either a low priority for Ottawa or have simply not figured at all in Canadian strategic concerns, except in the most indirect ways. However, these obstacles to ease of judgment pale in comparison to difficulties related to the speed of change in the hemisphere and in the world, dominating the last three or four years of international affairs and showing no signs of slowing down in the remainder of this century. In the past several years, we have seen much of the bedrock of the inter-American system simply swept away; it remains to be seen to what extent this lack of the traditional foundations for Western Hemispheric security cooperation will affect the future of security relations among its constituent states.

In this paper, the analysis will be attempted through a quick look at the past experience of the hemisphere in security matters, empha-sizing the period of the Cold War and underscoring recent changes in those issues. This new context will then be discussed in greater detail, bringing in the Canadian dimension. Subsequently, there will be an

---

Hal P. Klepak is with the Département d'études stratégiques, Collège militaire royal de Saint-Jean.

analysis of the sort of issues that are likely to arise in the field of security during the next few years, including some ideas of Canadian perceptions. A conclusion summarizes hemispheric defense challenges, given these new sets of problems, as well as a last word on a likely role for Canada.

Introduction

From the first discussions of hemispheric unity or Pan Americanism, defense and security have been at the forefront of the debate. The Liberators were well aware of the dangers of a European counterattack to restore Iberian powers' positions in continental Latin America in the years after independence, and the United States was alert to the potential disadvantages of this for its own policy and influence in the hemisphere.[1] The Monroe Doctrine as well as early Latin American attempts at unified military and even political fronts were reactions to this fear.[2]

The revolutions themselves left a tradition of cooperation for defense among the struggling new Spanish American regimes that needed each other in order to make real progress against the Spanish and the immensely powerful loyalist elements of their own populations. The Argentine effort in the liberation of Chile, the Grenadian experience in the North, and the joint efforts of Bolívar and San Martín to bring independence to Peru are only the most well known and successful of a large number of schemes for mutual assistance, ranging from Cuba and Mexico in the North to the bottom of the Southern Cone (González 1985).

Thus, solidarity was not new among the Latin American states as they moved into the mid-nineteenth century, a period in which, despite wars among themselves, there was at least some degree of cohesion in regional responses to outside intervention. This was especially evident during the 1860s for Peru in the face of Spanish pretensions and for Mexico in the case of French intervention in an ill-conceived imperial experiment. At the same time, there was also a growing perception of the need for Latin cohesion against U.S. designs in the region, especially after the 1846-1848 war with Mexico, filibustering attempts a decade later in Central America, and repeated interest in the acquisition of Cuba and Eastern Hispaniola.

As such, security remained a key concern throughout the hemisphere, but it tended to be seen in different ways. While European influence was to be kept out as much as possible for U.S. policy to succeed, such influence was welcomed in varying degrees by Latin Americans who usually felt it served as a useful counterbalance to Washington. As of the late 1880s when Pan Americanism began to take hold, apart from the peaceful settlement of disputes and the principle of non-intervention in hemispheric foreign policies, security issues did not find much common ground and were relegated to less serious discussion.

World War I saw some growth of inter-American defense cooperation, and, while this rarely had a true military element, the Panama Canal's 1914 opening demonstrated a greatly increased U.S. interest in Caribbean and, to some extent, South American security concerns. Showing the contradictory aspects of the Pan American defense union idea were the 1915 U.S. military intervention in Mexico and Brazil's participation in the war with the Central Powers alongside the United States — Brazil sent groups of officers and ships to serve with the United States, Royal Navies, and the Royal Air Force in war zones (Ferreira Vidrigal 1985). Much more frequent U.S. interventions in the Caribbean following the war stemmed from President Franklin D. Roosevelt's Good Neighbor Policy in the 1930s. This cooperative effort was well regarded by most Latin American nations and set the stage for closer cooperation during the Second World War. The diplomatic context for this cooperation was solidified by the 1928 establishment of the Pan American Union.

In the years immediately preceding the Japanese attack on Pearl Harbor, the bases for the inter-American security system were laid. First, U.S. pressure, combined with European weakness, led to American military missions replacing European ones as the source of guidance and influence for Central American armed forces. This trend had spread throughout Latin America by the time the United States declared war on Japan (Nunn 1985). The Spring 1940 fall of France and the Netherlands caused real concern in many hemispheric capitals that transfers of territory were imminent, bringing Axis power directly into the region. An inter-American defense scheme was set up, and joint planning and coordination of hemispheric defense efforts were established. The Pearl Harbor attack spurred increased cooperation in the Americas. By 1942 most Latin American nations responded to the call to honor previous agreements by regarding the Japanese attack on one American country as an attack on all. Outside the Southern Cone, supportive declarations of war were the order of the day. Lend-Lease had already been established with a number of cooperating countries, and arrangements allowed under this scheme led to a massive transfer of U.S. equipment to select Latin American countries. Accords for military bases in Brazil and most Caribbean countries complemented transfers of equipment and weaponry, and deals were cut for U.S. access to Latin American strategic minerals.[3] While the Brazilian infantry division sent to Italy was the only Latin American field formation to join the Allies, military cooperation was widespread, involving almost all hemispheric states by the end of the war.

The 1947 Rio Pact and the security arrangements of the OAS Charter of 1948 were made more permanent by the war-time situation. The Axis enemies were conveniently replaced by the Soviet Union as the Cold War gained steam, and Moscow easily replaced Berlin, Rome, and Tokyo as the foreign influence perceived to be attempting access to the Americas. The Korean War then put the capstone on the system through the Mutual Assistance Pacts (MAPs). These were bilateral accords between Washington and regional capitals that, in return for the provision of U.S. equipment, weapons, and training, gave the United States assured access to Latin American strategic minerals and other support in times of crisis.[4]

The system proved durable and helpful for U.S. security projects in the hemisphere. Washington was indeed able to consider its "backyard" secure and turn its full attention to global competition with the Soviet Union, untroubled by concerns about its rear (Varas 1988; Lafeber 1983). As the years passed, the system proved flexible as well. While it was difficult to take the idea of a direct Soviet military threat in the hemisphere seriously, it was much easier to consider the threat of communist subversion as real (Amaral Gurgel 1975; López 1987). Guatemala in 1954, and, in particular, Cuba in the early 1960s, provided possible examples, and the inter-American security system more than willingly took on more internal security-related tasks in response to the changed "threat." The inter-American system provided a blanket of legitimacy for the U.S. attempt to overthrow the Castro regime in Cuba as well as for the 1965 U.S. intervention in the Dominican Republic. Additionally, it provided the context for inter-American defense cooperation into the 1980s and helped to justify Washington's support for military regimes over much of the period (Queille 1969; Cortada and Cortada 1985).

Changes in the 1980s

Events of the last decade came close to shattering the inter-American security system. Even before 1980, with the decreasing diplomatic isolation of Cuba and the more independently minded foreign policies of several Latin American states, a trend toward less cohesion in the system was visible. However, the Falklands War affected the system most dramatically. When Argentina invaded the islands in early April 1982, despite widespread Latin American cynicism expressed privately and not so privately about Argentine claims, the bulk of official Latin American reaction expressed the expectation that the United States would side with Buenos Aires given the obligations of the Rio Treaty. However, U.S. reluctance to break openly with the United Kingdom was also understood to a great extent. What was less comprehensible was Washington's eventual siding with London and even cooperating, although much less than many Argentine sources claim, with the British war effort. Latin American countries with somewhat similar axes to grind (for example, Guatemala with Belize and Venezuela with Guyana) loudly denounced the U.S. position, and many others also declared the end of the inter-American security system (Varas 1988).

As if this were not serious enough, U.S. determination to topple the Sandinista government in Nicaragua after 1981 and its refusal to cooperate with Latin American attempts to bring peace to Central America further divided the system. U.S. attitudes provided the impetus for the creation of groups like Contadora, the Rio Group, and the Group of Eight. Clearly, their goal was to develop policies free from U.S. input and control.[5]

In addition, Washington's use of a multilateral forum to end the leftist regime in Grenada in 1983, although not directly related to OAS or Rio Treaty provisions, brought back the worst memories and suspicions about U.S. designs in the region. The 1989 invasion of Panama simply reminded many Latin Americans about the lack of U.S. interest in an inter-American system based on the equality of status among its members. It also reinforced Washington's continued determination to use the existing system to forward exclusive U.S. policies.[6]

None of these regional incidents had the same effect on the system as the demise of the Soviet Union. Continuation of all the arrangements established during the Second World War, of the Rio Treaty, and of the OAS Charter was premised on a Soviet threat. When that threat could not be justified by conventional military analysis, it was converted to an ideological one. The Soviet ideological menace was considered as particularly dangerous because of the arrival in the hemisphere of Fidel Castro's communist regime, a supposed Soviet surrogate.

With the end of the Soviet empire in Eastern Europe and the collapse of the "mother country of socialism" itself, the raison d'être of the whole inter-American security system logically was called into question. Disarmament became the watchword, and the world moved into a unipolar stage, the length of which depends not only on Washington but also on Tokyo and Bonn/Brussels.

The New Context

The early 1990s present a completely new context for the inter-American security system and probably for the inter-American system as a whole. With the exception of the Cuban regime, a serious threat surely only to itself, and the wild Sendero Luminoso movement in Peru, there are no major forces in the Western Hemisphere adhering to the ideological line that had justified the inter-American system since the late 1940s, and, more specifically, since 1962. In neither case is there any support from the former Soviet Union for these movements. Indeed, Sendero Luminoso considers itself the vanguard of a new stage of communist revolution and has made little effort to hide its hatred for the former leadership of the former Soviet Union. It is only slightly less vitriolic in its denunciations of the government in Beijing (Hertoghe and Lebrousse 1989). Cuba is suffering from the end of Soviet military assistance and feels an ever-growing economic pinch since former members of the Soviet Union began trading exclusively on the basis of mutually beneficial barter trade or hard currency exchange.[7]

There is no significant threat from the historic menace of the past four and a half decades. Yet, the obvious fact remains that the whole infrastructure of the inter-American security system is still in place. The Rio Treaty still holds full formal validity and has not been denounced by any signatory, not even Cuba or Nicaragua. The security provisions of the OAS Charter have not been removed nor in any way revised. The Inter-American Defense Board and the Inter-American Defense College continue to function in Washington. Bilateral basing arrangements are maintained throughout the Americas, without a rush to abrogate the Mutual Assistance Pacts. Finally, joint annual conferences of

American navies, air forces, and armies continue to take place on a regular basis. Training for Latin American forces proceeds in a wide variety of fields and in many U.S. military schools and installations.

If many things appear to have remained the same, however, these surface appearances cover a completely altered strategic reality not only in the East-West context but also within the region. Most dramatic, perhaps, has been the virtual surrender of Argentina to Brazil in their one hundred seventy-year-old struggle for preeminence in South America. This rivalry, the bedrock of much post-independence intra-regional diplomacy, has been replaced by cooperation in fields as different as electricity and commerce and as sensitive as defense and nuclear energy development.[8] While Argentina is very much the junior partner in this cooperative effort, the usual high standard of foreign policy on the part of Brazil's Itamaraty (foreign ministry) has meant that Buenos Aires has had to suffer little humiliation as a result.

U.S.-Mexican relations have been turned upside down by the development of a completely new attitude by the Mexican leadership, which, after the shock of a decade of economic nightmares, accepted that it could no longer favor questions of sovereignty and indepen-dence at the expense of foreign investment and close economic relations with the United States (Reynolds and Wager 1990). NAFTA negotiations are the culmination of this process which has already seen decades of Mexican diplomatic tradition replaced by a cooperative approach on a wide range of issues previously known as thorny sources of dispute between the two countries.

As mentioned earlier, Cuba's privileged relations with the Soviet Union are now obviously a thing of the past. Nicaragua's government is now solidly pro-Western, and, although the FSLN remains the strongest single political force, there is little doubt that the return of a Sandinista government in Managua would be fraught with none of the difficulties of East-West relations that hampered its U.S. relationship until February 1990.

The end of the civil war in El Salvador and the negotiations occurring between government and rebels in Guatemala also suggest that a general peace is not far away in Central America.[9] This will, no doubt, mean that the region assumes less importance for the United States and will certainly no longer "Centralamericanize" Washington's relations with Latin America as a whole.

The return of civilian governments to almost all Latin American countries will facilitate their relations with the United States and temper misunderstandings between Washington and a number of Latin American states. While there is no guarantee that this state of affairs will long remain, as witnessed by the coup attempts in Caracas, for the time being democracy seems to be making some headway in the entire region. This must signal a change in U.S.-Latin American relations.

Negotiations on outstanding issues and the military cooperation of Bolivia, Chile, and Peru with Venezuela and Colombia seem to augur well for better relations among and between those countries. In any case, economic reality is forcing almost all the region's states to move closer toward economic cooperation and bridge-building among themselves, thus reducing the importance of their historic rivalries and disagreements. The end of military governments has, in many ways, aided this change, as less nationalistic forces came to control domestic and foreign policies.

Drugs have begun to dominate U.S.-Latin American security relations to an extent undreamt of only a few years ago. The preference among some sectors in Washington for a military response to this problem has meant considerable pressure on Latin American, particularly Andean, countries to use their forces to combat the drug trade in cooperation with those of the United States (Mabry 1989). While the recent discussions in San Antonio seem to have put the military on a back burner, this is not necessarily a situation which will last.

Overall, it is difficult to avoid the conclusion that the inter-American security world is a very different place now, even though some historically visible elements appear to remain very much in place, unchanged by the events of recent years. Nonetheless, it is equally tempting to think that this is a result of the difficulties of addressing relevant issues once they are formally raised by any or all the members of the system. If there is no longer a threat, as some have already asked, why maintain the system at all? Others suggest that the only threat left is that of U.S. intervention and that, therefore, there should be a Latin American-only security system to deal with this problem (Portales 1987). Still others maintain that there is room to use the inter-American security system to do things other than counter the former Soviet threat and that decision makers should be thinking of a system that confronts military or drug trafficking threats to democratic regimes and/or any threats to the environment (Mercado Jarrin 1989). Whether such a system should include the United States, much less be led by it, or should be merely South American, not Latin American (given Mexico's evolving situation) — all are questions being asked in Latin America and the United States. Given the potential for discord and misunderstanding, it is surely not surprising to see governments less than anxious to open this particular Pandora's box.

The View from Canada

It must first be admitted that hemispheric defense, as a concept, has never held much attraction for Ottawa and has rarely had much of a hearing in Canadian security circles. For good or ill, Canadians have been content to remain aloof from defense considerations affecting Latin America. Canadian defense interests in the region have been seen as minimal or even nonexistent. While the Royal Canadian Navy did put ashore a small landing party in El Salvador in the 1930s to protect British subjects threatened by the local insurrection, and whereas some Canadian infantry battalions were deployed during the war to relieve regular British units in British Honduras and a number of the Empire's possessions in the West Indies, Canadian National Defense Headquarters has traditionally considered the entire hemisphere south of the Rio Grande to be an exclusive area of U.S. interest. This became even more evident following the Second World War (MacKenzie 1991). Even well before World War II, the end of British competition with the United States in the region was self-evident, and hence Canadian defense concerns there were also viewed as peripheral.

This must be considered in the proper context. As a member of the British Empire, Canada was excluded from the early and middle stages of the development of the Pan American idea, its eventual union, and, to some extent, from the OAS. Ottawa was viewed by Washington as a potential Trojan Horse, bringing British influence into the Americas, just as the United States was forging an instrument specifically designed to keep out European influence. To a great extent, this was perfectly logical (Humphreys 1981). It must be remembered that until 1939 the most likely threat for which Canadian defense-planning was made was the United States, although the likelihood of a U.S. attack steadily diminished throughout the century. Canadian military history until 1899 was one of defense against the threat from the South, and while the Boer War and World War I were fought against menaces much farther afield, Canadian participation was basically felt as a sort of payment of dues by Canada. It was the only part of the Empire possessing a land border with a great power, and it hoped the other parts of the Empire would come to Canada's future aid if necessary (English 1991; Morton 1985).

World War II changed all of that. During the war, the fall of continental Europe made the threat to both Britain and Canada real. Cooperation with the United States began even before the full collapse of France, and Canada's involvement in the war at Britain's side made Prime Minister MacKenzie King anxious to reassure its powerful neighbor that Canadian land, sea, and air space would never be used by a third party for an attack on the United States. Other promises followed and were underscored by U.S. assistance with and eventual participation in the war against the Axis in ways that heightened Canadian-American joint operations in defense (Granatstein 1977).

While still barred from the Pan American Union and, after 1940, from discussions of hemispheric defense affecting areas south of the United States, Canada was far from seriously troubled by this state of affairs. It was busy in the North Atlantic and with its cooperation in the Commonwealth war effort. Cooperation with the United States was strictly bilateral or based on Anglo-American accords involving Commonwealth participation.

After the war, joint U.S.-Canadian defense arrangements continued in many spheres. However, a dimension south of the Rio Grande was never proposed by either side. While continental accords were signed with the United States for North American defense, the Caribbean and South America were simply ignored. Canada showed no interest in either signing the Rio Treaty or joining the emerging full-blown inter-American system, political or military.[10] As confirmed by Canada's placing of the State Department in the Western Europe section of the Foreign Ministry, it simply did not consider itself an American nation (Arciniegas 1985; Ogelsby 1976).

While the 1950s heightened Canada's strategic value to the United States, especially as the routes for developing Soviet bomber and, eventually, missile forces mostly passed over the Dominion to reach U.S. targets, this situation did not lead to greater Canadian interest in considering hemispheric defense as a logical place to devote resources. Rather, Europe and the very comfortable North Atlantic Alliance received the greatest priority, as it included both mother countries, the bulk of the world's democracies, and a means of maintaining multilateral relations with the United States, a posture which was very much in favor in Ottawa. Latin America was not discussed in defense terms despite very close North American defense cooperation, culminating in the 1958 NORAD accords.

It must also be said that the general Canadian perception of the inter-American security system was that it was dominated by the United States and full of slightly unsavory military governments with which Canada had little in common. Military cooperation was not considered, and, despite the importance of the military in many Latin American countries, Canada's increasing number of embassies in the region did not include a single military attaché.[11] The Latin American military was a clearly distrusted element for many years.

Canada's experience with the United States in Latin America was often a source of disagreement. Canada was not forthcoming with support for Washington when the Jacobo Arbenz regime was over-thrown in Guatemala during 1954; Ottawa also did not approve of the 1965 Dominican Republic intervention. Even more dramatic were Canada's continuing good relations with Cuba after the establishment of the Fidel Castro regime. Indeed, this situation laid the groundwork for a very serious dispute with the United States during the 1962 Missile Crisis when Prime Minister John Diefenbaker's feathers were more than a bit ruffled by what he saw as toadying to the United States on the defense cooperation front (Jockel 1987; Ogelsby 1976).

The 1980s changed everything. In the early 1970s, the Liberal government of Pierre Trudeau had already begun to show much more interest in Latin America as part of Trudeau's "third option" proposals. While far from tempted by military cooperation with Latin America at a time when civilian governments were yielding with increasing rapidity to the proponents of the Doctrine of National Security, Mr. Trudeau did launch some initiatives which, at least, made Latin America slightly better known to Canadians. However, the key change awaited the growth of Canadian interest in Central America in the 1980s.

Canada had always tended to believe that the roots of insurgency in Latin America lay in socioeconomic problems and not in the East-West struggle. In Central America, Canada's assessment of the problem was bound to differ markedly from Washington's. Ottawa felt it could help in the resolution of the region's civil wars, and it was concerned that Washington's fixation on the "communist" challenge in the area prevented it from applying deserved attention to more vital problems on the world scene (Cirincione 1985). Fortunately, this view was also shared by two other close U.S. allies — Spain and West Germany. Be that as it may, there had also been an extraordinary growth in Canadian NGOs active in Central America. This constituency found a domestic public increasingly caught up in the region's difficulties, and the Ottawa government was obliged to listen as public opinion called for increasing Canadian action.[12]

The result was a forward policy toward Central America with eventual help on the security front, principally with peacekeeping advice and planning assistance. Canadian military officers actually went to Central America and worked with their counterparts and insurgents in the area. In connection with the Contadora initiative, which was strongly supported by Canada, Canadian officers were active in ways meant to increase in scope once UN interests began to be deployed to Central America. When the UN actually sent a reconnaissance group and a full-blown verification and peacekeeping force in late 1989, Canada was the most highly represented country, with scores of officers and a squadron of helicopters.[13]

In 1990 Canada became a member of the OAS, although the government has been careful to insist that it will not sign the Rio Treaty and has added a reservation stating it will not be bound by articles in the OAS Charter dealing with security affairs (Klepak 1990). Nonetheless, with the Central American experience, the Canadian military has now worked with its Latin American counterparts, has improved its Spanish-language ability, has gained knowledge of the area and its problems, and is now represented by a military attaché in Mexico City (responsible for Cuba and Central America).

Thus, the country has moved from a determined distancing from security considerations in the region to a point where there is a clear security dimension to Canada's membership in the OAS, even if not yet formal. It should also be said that Ottawa in its short term has been active in the hemispheric organization in areas related to security, such as disarmament, peaceful resolution of disputes, democratization, control of the military in order to reduce the chance of military coups, and peacekeeping (DEA 1991).[14]

None of this, however, changes the fact that the essential concerns of Canadian defense remain those related to the country's geographic position, sharing the North American continent with the

United States. The European dimension of the defense posture has been reduced in the wake of the end of the Cold War, and the relative importance of Canada's efforts toward continental defense has greatly increased. The Commonwealth provides a diminishing security interest for Canada, although it has hardly disappeared as a context for defense activity. Some of its defense aspects closely touch the Caribbean, some of whose forces are partly trained by Canada. Francophone Canada never really had a defense aspect for historical and political reasons. With Europe lessening as a defense priority, continental defense becomes almost all-important, leading to dangers for the Canadian tradition of multilateralism. It is in this context that Canadian security cooperation with Latin America may increase in the next decade.

Likely Issues of the 1990s

When asking what the likely security issues of the 1990s will be, the question must be raised, "Security interests of whom?" As mentioned earlier, security matters generally, and certainly in this hemisphere, are not clear-cut and reflect the position of the analyst. As the Cold War ends, it becomes clear that Washington has different views about what constitute security issues than do Mexico City, Brasilia, Buenos Aires, Havana, or even Ottawa. The view expressed here will be Canadian, even though the nature of the issue tends to link any Canadian view to U.S. perspectives. It will also be indicated where Canadian concerns may be shared with Latin American states.

It must be said that Canada's defense policy is principally shaped by its status as a middle power bordering on the greatest power in the world — a nation whose relative power has increased immeasurably since the victorious end of its rivalry with the Soviet Union. Canadian defense priorities have revolved for decades around defending North America in cooperation with the United States, contributing to collective defense through NATO, ensuring Canadian sovereignty over national territory and waters, and contributing to world stability through peacekeeping. Not surprisingly, the first of these priorities has involved defense cooperation with the United States. There is no doubt that this will continue to be the cornerstone of defense policy and that no other policy would make geopolitical sense (Bergeron 1989). Indeed, most trends point to the North American dimension of national defense assuming a higher priority than it has ever known.

In this context, U.S. reactions to what it perceives as security problems are a factor in Canada's own perceptions of threat, whether or not it shares Washington's views on the same matters. In the following section of this paper, the basic feature of a small power's defense relations maintained in the shadow of a superpower's defenses must be taken into consideration.

Instability

There is little doubt that Canada, like the United States, wants to see stability in the rest of the hemisphere, even if that stability is seen in a somewhat different manner than the dominant U.S. view. Instability can lead to disorder and destruction which can, in turn, result in situations causing massive emigration and other problems that have a habit of becoming international via their transborder ramifications. Canadian governments are, of course, interested in the safety of national investments, trade, and citizens abroad, but the impact of instability in other areas can be even more serious.

Related to instability and disruption of trade is the issue of access to strategic minerals. Much was made of this some years ago during the successive oil crises, although of late it is not often discussed. This is particularly true of a mineral-rich nation, such as Canada. The country imports significant amounts of tungsten, nickel, and platinum, and Latin America is the only key for access to bauxite and tin. It is easy to exaggerate this importance. In real terms, the only serious concerns voiced in the recent past about strategic imports are oil-related.[15] Venezuela is a particularly impressive oil exporter to Canada, especially when seen as part of the triangular relationship involving U.S.-Canadian accords on the intra-North American petroleum trade. Disruptions of these arrangements could be troublesome and could include a security dimension (Klepak 1990, 192).

Drugs

More serious is another sort of trade, this time illicit. The impact of the illegal drug trade on U.S. relations with countries such as Mexico, Colombia, Peru, and Bolivia has been considerable, leading to accusations that those relations have been kidnapped by the narcotrafficking problem (del Villar 1989). U.S. policy on the issue has concentrated overwhelmingly on the supposed faults of the producer countries, while minimizing domestic efforts to curb consumption or, in the case of marijuana, even production. In addition, the emphasis on destruction of production has meant often strident calls for the producing countries to employ their military forces and to allow for U.S. force deployment in Latin American countries in the so-called "war" on drugs, and to do so with ever greater vigor (Mabry 1989; Lowenthal 1987).

The militarization of the drug war has occurred also in the United States itself where the National Guard, Army, Air Force, and Navy have been added to the assets of the Drug Enforcement Agency and Customs Service (not to mention various levels of police forces) assets in a bid to defeat the trade. The armed forces — at first, extremely uninterested in any such role — have found that with the end of the Cold War, there is much to commend the anti-drug role in terms of budget retention and popularity with the public (Bagley 1989; Lane 1992).

This is not the case in Latin America. While the armed forces in Mexico have long been involved in various anti-contraband operations — and the drug war fits neatly into such traditional roles — in Peru and, to some extent, in Colombia, the use of the military against the drug lords means that resources are deployed away from the very real fight against domestic insurgency. Indeed, as seen in Peru, the fight against the drug producers may be highly counterproductive in the effort to defeat insurgency (Moral 1989; García Sayá 1989).

The United States has declared the threat of drugs to American society as the number one security problem faced by the nation now that the Soviet threat is over.[16] In reaction, Mexico has done the same, even though its problem is not so much domestic use as the dangers of overreaction on the part of the United States.[17]

The practice of certifying national governments for the seriousness of their efforts against drugs in order to permit them access to U.S. aid means that priority is placed on this struggle above all other aspects of U.S. policy in the hemisphere (del Villar 1989). Even Canada has felt some pressure for more action on the drug front, and it is conceivable that this pressure could increase as our "soft border" with the United States becomes progressively softer and as Latin American efforts to disrupt the trade bear fruit farther south. The military is already slightly involved in countering the trade, and this role is expected to grow (Klepak 1990).

In this context, Canada will probably continue to press for further international efforts to deal with the trade, while continuing to feel that military means avail little in this area. In fact, this tends to poison the atmosphere for dealing with other major problems needing solutions. If the United States continues to see the problem as one of security, it is not certain that Canada will be able to resist accepting the Mexican route on this issue of militarization.

Democratization and the Role of the Military

Democratization does not automatically strike Canadians as a security issue. Nonetheless, the links between democratization and Canada's role in the hemisphere are probably greater than first meet the eye. There is little doubt that Canada was able to join the OAS on January 1, 1990, because the governments of the region were more democratic than they had been for many decades. Given Canada's Central American experience, Canada could play a more useful role in a largely democratic Western Hemisphere.

Canada's position is that the strengthening of regional democracies should be a prime role of the OAS, supported by all countries in the hemisphere. [Former] Prime Minister Mulroney has spoken of the increased linkage between democratization and the kind of aid Canadians are prepared to give a country and its government. The return of military governments in Latin America, a frighteningly real prospect, would be extremely damaging to the government's intentions to bring Canada closer to its Latin American partners. The recently reduced military role in the region has led to much frustration among some of the countries' officer corps. It is important to keep in mind that with the exception of Nicaragua, former military dictatorships of other regional countries were never really ousted from power but surrendered under their own conditions and often on their own timetables (Klepak 1986; Rizzo de Oliveira 1987). Canada wants to see democracy sustained throughout the hemisphere. Its policy toward Haiti and its keenness for better means of applying OAS pressure on recalcitrant regimes demonstrate this interest.

The Canadian government considers military governments to be more prone to adventurism of the Falklands War type, and it perceives international tension as providing armed forces a greater raison d'être for rallying support for a military regime as well as a means of raising defense budgets. Therefore, a reduction in the role of the armed forces in Latin American countries will be an important defense-related aspect of Canadian policy in the region.

Peacekeeping and the Peaceful Settlement of Disputes

There is little doubt that Canadians believe, with their unique experience in peacekeeping and quiet diplomacy, that they can be of assistance in the peaceful settlement of regional disputes. There is a long tradition of debate, diplomatic discussion, treaty signing, and large-scale ignoring of commitments concerning the peaceful settlement of Latin American disputes.[18] However, it is difficult to imagine an international context with more success in this area. Many initiatives are being launched for arms control, disarmament, and negotiations of various confidence-building measures within Latin America (Palma 1986, 62-74).

Canada's attitude toward the OAS and the UN will be colored by their evolution toward peaceful settlement of disputes. Before the Central American peacekeeping and verification deployment, the UN was largely absent from the Latin American scene with respect to peaceful dispute settlement. This conforms with U.S. preferences on the matter (Klepak 1990a, 44). This context may well be changing, not only because of more UN resolve but also because of a much more pro-UN attitude on the part of the U.S. government.

Canada will wish to be very active in this area, as it has been in bringing to the OAS issues of disarmament, arms control, and confidence-building measures. Being the newcomer on the block may have advantages in this regard.

In military peacekeeping operations, Canada is very well placed. Despite a lack of language skills for Latin American duties, the Armed Forces are the most experienced in the world in this field and offer unique advantages in command and control, communications, logistics, and many other areas (Granatstein 1991). Additionally, in an era of increasing continentalism, there will be many in Ottawa who view the chance for the Canadian military to operate outside North America as being extremely favorable to Canadian national and military objectives with respect to multilateralism.

In the past, a concern of great importance would have been nuclear proliferation. After the recent accords between Buenos Aires and Brasilia in this regard, however, there is much less worry in Ottawa. The return of military regimes or more nationalistic governments to either of those countries would, on the other hand, have to be carefully examined and would be a source of serious Canadian concern, especially given its early role in the Argentine nuclear program.[19]

Related to this is missile technology. Canada is very involved in the current drive to limit the proliferation of technologies helpful in the construction of ballistic missile systems. Brazil is still active in this area, although its programs are claimed to be largely space-research oriented. Argentina's abandonment of the Condor missile program is still raising questions in some circles (Avignolo 1991, 2). Other countries are not far away from significant capabilities in this field. Ottawa is ready to suggest initiatives both in this area and in the general area of arms sales. Given the importance of the Brazilian and Argentine arms industries, there may be scope for disagreement in this respect.

Cuba

The idea that Cuba constitutes any real threat to hemispheric security is regarded as ridiculous in Ottawa, as it is elsewhere in NATO. It is, however, an observable fact that Cuba's recent desperation has been accompanied not by a softening of Washington's opposition to it but rather by a hardening of the U.S. position in treatment of the island republic (Jenkins 1991, 197). Canada maintains good relations with Havana; however, it would like to see changes in the regime.

At the moment, Ottawa finds itself in line with the views of the majority of Latin American states, although this could change. It is conceivable that Washington will be able to orchestrate a more negative policy on the part of more Latin American nations now that its hand has been strengthened by so many factors on the international scene. Any such attempt would be resisted by Ottawa, where its Cuba policy has been constant through Liberal and Conservative governments alike for a third of a century. Indeed, Ottawa is anxious to play a more active role in reintegrating Cuba into the inter-American family, and this has been recommended by a parliamentary committee looking into the matter.

The Panama Canal

The Panama Canal has been considered by virtually all U.S. administrations as a vital national interest since it was first opened nearly eight decades ago. Many of the basic arrangements made elsewhere in the Americas have been explained as part of a system of approaches to the canal. U.S. military and diplomatic interventions in several countries, over the last half century and more, have been justified by the "security" of the canal.

In wartime the canal has also been important for Canada. During the first years of the Second World War, ships from the main Pacific base at Esquimalt used the canal to shorten the Atlantic voyage to Halifax. This process was reversed at the end of that war and later during the Korean war. It is difficult to assess the extent to which a Canadian mobilization in support of NATO Europe would have been dependent on the availability of the canal, but there is no doubt that its value was considerable in that strategic context.[20]

With the end of the Cold War, however, there are more doubts about the canal's strategic importance to Canada and, indeed, even to the United States. South of the border its importance is now a matter of faith, whereas further north this is far from being the case. In Latin America the canal is regarded as a potentially explosive issue.

Most Latin American countries criticized the United States sharply over the 1989 invasion of Panama. While some of this was, no doubt, tongue-in-cheek (Noriega being anything but popular), there was equally no doubt that Latin Americans did not appreciate yet another precedent for U.S. intervention, this time the war on drugs (Klepak 1990a). Also a subject of much adverse comment is the dismantling of the Panamanian National Guard by U.S. occupying authorities, which seized those weapons claimed to have made that force generally capable of defending the canal in case of attack. Since the treaty obliging the United States to withdraw from the Canal Zone at the end of the century conditions that withdrawal on the existence of a force in Panama capable of taking on the task of canal defense, it is easy to believe cynics in Latin America and elsewhere (Klepak 1990a, 106).

A Security System for the 1990s

While there are many traditional security issues that will confront Canada, the United States, and Latin America in the 1990s, it is certainly in the area of the inter-American security system itself that the major questions will arise. As mentioned, the historic raison d'être of the system has been abandoned and is unlikely to reappear with any major force.

The reworking of the system will not, however, just compete with the obvious obstacles of vested interests. There are major questions which are still constantly posed, such as should the inter-American security system remain at all and if not, what should replace it? If so, should it be an alliance against disorder and change or against anti-democratic forces? Should it be against the drug trade or, perhaps, pollution? Should it be, according to some, a combination of these new areas of security interests? Should it be replaced by a system simply Latin American or even South American? Should it merely be a more effective framework for the peaceful resolution of disputes, one aimed at capitalizing on progress currently being made to reduce the size and power of the armed forces in Latin America?[21]

These are complicated and, in many cases, frightening prospects, and they have been largely ignored at governmental levels. Nonetheless, they are not disappearing. It is likely that there will be a reworking of the inter-American security system, and its nature will change drastically. At the same time, the relatively stronger United States may seek to retain more of the old system than might seem logical to many observers.

What is certain is that no Canadian government will be interested in participating in a regional security system which excludes the United States. There is no perception of a sufficiently high level of common security interest between Canada and Latin America to make a joint security system sensible, especially if this were, in some extraordinary way, viewed as aimed at the United States. While some of the issues raised by Latin Americans (about the need for a hemispheric security system aimed at combating pollution, drugs, anti-democratic movements, and other "new" security problems) would possibly be of interest to Canada, the presence of the United States in such a system, even with the concomitant threat of its dominance, would be preferable to one from which it was absent.

Canadians would agree that there are elements of the new and old that apply to any threat perception related to the hemisphere. Still, they would probably prefer that current arrangements were maintained, especially vis-à-vis North America and, to some extent, toward South America. However, if a new hemispheric system is worked out, it is conceivable that Canada would participate, particularly if it addressed Canada-relevant issues and promoted continued democracy in Latin America.

The environment is a serious issue for Canadians; drugs are as well. However, in the author's view, there is a salutary dose of skepticism as to the good sense of including such problems as security issues. They have aspects which, no doubt, can be seen in this way. In Canada as in Mexico, there is considerable reluctance to call everything a security issue simply because it attracts more money from governments. The danger is that the temptation will exist to raise the profile of many issues by calling them security issues, and one will no longer be clear on what constitutes an actual security concern (Elguea 1989).

On the issue of democracy, Canadians are most concerned that there may be a return to military regimes in Latin America if there is no escape from the current world economic crisis within the next few years. Canada would probably be willing to participate in many types of joint efforts, short of military action, to dissuade national armed forces from intervening against their constitutional masters. However, there would surely be no interest in military engagements that would require the Canadian Forces to take part in joint interventions in order to save democracy in foreign states. That would be a departure from the Canadian diplomatic tradition of non-interference in other states' internal affairs. Such interference would be difficult to sell to the Canadian public, however well-motivated the system members were.

Conclusions

Canada is now an official part of the Americas, even if it has not joined the hemisphere's formal security system. The current government and opposition parties have agreed that Latin American links should be strengthened as part of a long-standing multilateral tradition of foreign policy. Those particular links have, however, already been strengthened in a number of ways with respect to hemispheric security matters. This has meant, as expected by many analysts, that it would be difficult to stay entirely out of the security field once Canada joined the OAS.

Canada recognizes that there are threats to security in the Americas that can impact Canada, even if only indirectly. It agrees that there are possible hemispheric responses to a number of problems which can be linked to national security, even if the Canadian tradition is not to do so.

With the disappearance of the traditional threat to the hemisphere, issues of democracy, the environment, drug interdiction, and general disorder are often added to those related to more usual defense analysis. With the exception of initiatives in the area of the peaceful settlement of disputes, support for democracy, peacekeeping, and perhaps drugs and immigration, Canada is unlikely to have a forward policy on hemispheric security matters. However, it will have preferences about the way current security arrangements are re-structured. The reform or dismantling of the inter-American security system will largely be a subject for U.S.-Latin American debate. This is the challenge on the 1990s security agenda in at least the southern portion of the hemisphere, and it has received very little attention in Ottawa. Until now, Canadian attention has been firmly focused on the rapidly evolving situation in North America, and what is happening there has all but precluded concern with the South. Thus, Canada, while still a member of the inter-American community, is kept from automatically linking its own security problems with those of its new partners in the Americas by a considerable force of tradition.

Notes

[1] See Pierre Queille, 1969, *L'Amérique latine, la doctrine Monroe et le panaméricanisme* (Paris: Payot) for a lengthy discussion of this policy assessment.

[2] This is not to say, however, that Latin American and U.S. statesmen saw the situation in the same light. If the former were concerned about European political intentions in the region, they were not without worries about those of Washington either.

[3] See Jan Knippers-Black, 1982, *Sentinels of Empire* (New York: Green-wood) for a more detailed discussion of this entire process. For Brazil, see Nelson Werneck Sodré, 1979, *A Historia militar do Brasil* (Rio de Janeiro: Civilização brasileira), 323-326.

[4] See Lars Schoultz, 1987, *National Security and United States Policy toward Latin America* (Princeton: Princeton University Press). For a highly critical account of the MAPs, see Horacio Veneroni, 1973, *Estados Unidos y las fuerzas armadas en América Latina* (Buenos Aires: Periferia).

[5] See the numerous points of view on this subject in Cristina Eguizábal, ed., 1988, *América Latina y la crisis centroamericana: en busca de una solución regional* (Buenos Aires: GEL).

[6] For a longer discussion of Panama-related issues since the invasion, see this author's chapter on the canal in H.P. Klepak, 1990, *Canada and Latin America: Strategic Issues for the 1990s* (Ottawa: ORAE).

[7] For a series of points of view on this issue, see H.M. Axelman and John Kirk, 1991, *Cuban Foreign Policy Confronts a New International Order* (Boulder: Lynne Rienner). For the specific defense aspects of this issue, see Hal P. Klepak, 1991, "Hard Times Ahead for Havana," *Jane's Defense Weekly*, October 12, 666-668.

[8] For discussions of different aspects of the Brazilian-Argentine rapprochement, see Roberto Russell, 1990, "Argentina: ¿una nueva política exterior?" 20-22, and Magdalena Segue and Héctor E. Bocco, "Brasil: el fin de temporada," 32-35, both in *El Desafío de los '90*, ed. Heraldo Muñoz (Caracas: Nueva Sociedad, 1990); and Hal P. Klepak, 1992, "Le tango de la dénucléarisation: le duo Argentine et Brásil," in *La Prolifération nucléaire dans les années 1990,* eds. Albert Legault and Michel Fortmann (Québec: Centre québécois de relations internationales, 1992).

[9] For a discussion of problems that persist, see Hal P. Klepak, "Remaining Obstacles to Peace in Central America," 1992, *Notes Stratégiques* No.2, (St. Jean: The Queen's Printer).

[10] See Germán Arciniegas, 1985, *OEA: La Suerte de una organización regional* (Bogotá: Planeta) for several chapters dealing with this state of affairs.

For background to this, see J.C.M. Ogelsby, 1976, *Gringos from the Far North* (Toronto: Macmillan).

11 There had been several requests for such attachés made by the Department of External Affairs, the argument running that such officers would have better access to the corridors of power than would civilian diplomats. None were answered favorably until the summer of 1991 when a first defense attaché was sent to Mexico.

12 For a lengthy analysis of the myriad aspects of this trend's evolution, see Liisa North, 1990, *Between War and Peace in Central America: Choices for Canada*, (Toronto: Between the Lines).

13 For details of this operation, see "ONUCA OBSERVER," 1991, Tegucigalpa: Lithopress.

14 For the range of issues involved, see Carlos Moneta, 1990, "Pensamiento y acción latinoamericana ante las fuerzas armadas. Percepciones, conductas tradicionales y nuevas alternativas" in the same author's edited volume, *Civiles y militares: fuerzas armadas y transición democrática* (Caracas: Nueva Sociedad), 21-22.

15 For more on the minerals issue, and especially oil, see Jock Finlayson, 1989, "Canada as a Strategic Mineral Importer: the Problematical Minerals," in *The New Geopolitics of Minerals,* ed. David Haglund (Vancouver: University of British Columbia Press).

16 National Security Decision Directive Number 221, discussed in Mark Hertling, 1990, "Narcoterrorism, the New Unconventional War," *Military Review* (March), 16-28.

17 This point is convincingly argued in Maria Celia Toro, 1989, "Mexico y Estados Unidos: El narcotráfico como amenaza a la seguridad nacional." In *En busca de la seguridad perdida. Aproximaciones a la seguridad nacional mexicana,* eds. Sergio Aguayo Quezada and Bruce M. Bagley (Mexico: Siglo Vientíuno), 367-87.

18 Hugo Palma, 1986, *América Latina: Limitación de armamentos y desarme en la región* (Lima: CEPEI) 60-62, has probably the best work on this subject to date.

19 See the last section and conclusion of the excellent unpublished thesis of Dean Martins, 1990, "Non-proliferation Policy and Nuclear Threshold States: The Case of Argentina and Brazil" (Kingston: Queen's University).

20 To some extent, the comments made by Lars Schoultz, 1987, *National Security and the United States Policy Toward Latin America* (Princeton: Princeton University Press) on the strictly military side of this matter can be transferred from the United States to Canada, always remembering that Canadian action in this area was not that of a world power (although during World War II it was not far from that status).

[21] The best discussions of these issues are found in the works of two key authors on security matters in Latin America: Edgardo Mercado Jarrin and Augusto Varas. A reflection of the views of both can be found in the former's 1987, "Perspectivas de los acuerdos de limitación y desarme en América Latina y el Caribe," and the latter's 1987, "De la Competencia a la Cooperación Militar en América Latina," both of which are found in *Paz, desarme y desarrollo en América Latina,* ed. Augusto Varas (Buenos Aires: GEL). See also Edgardo Mercado Jarrin, 1989, *Un Sistema de Seguridad y Defensa Sudamericano* (Lima: CONCYTEC) and Carlos Portales, 1987, "Seguridad regional en Sudamérica. Escenarios prospectivos," in *Paz, desarme y desarrollo en América Latina*, ed. Augusto Varas (Buenos Aires: GEL).

References

Arciniegas, Germán. 1985. *OEA: La suerte de una organización regional.* Bogotá: Planeta.

Amaral Gurgel, José A. 1975. *Segurança e democracia.* Rio de Janeiro: Biblioteca do Exército.

Avignolo, Maria Laura. 1991. "Death of the Argentine 'Condor'." *Latinamerica Press.* June 6.

Axelman, H. M., and John Kirk. 1991. *Cuban Foreign Policy Confronts a New International Order.* Boulder: Lynne Rienner.

Bagley, Bruce M. 1989. "The New Hundred Years War?: U.S. National Security and the War on Drugs in Latin America." In *The Latin American Narcotics Trade and U.S. National Security,* ed. Donald J. Mabry. New York: Greenwood.

Bergeron, Claude, et al. 1989. *Les choix géopolitiques du Canada: l'enjeu de la neutralité.* Montreal: Méridien.

Cirincione, Joseph, ed. 1985. *Central America and the Western Alliance.* New York: Holmes and Meier.

Cortada, James N., and James W. Cortada. 1985. *U.S. Foreign Policy in the Caribbean, Cuba and Central America.* New York: Praeger.

del Villar, Samuel I. 1989. "Rethinking Hemispheric Antinarcotics Strategy and Security." In *The Latin American Narcotics Trade and U.S. National Security,* ed. Donald J. Mabry. New York: Greenwood.

Department of External Affairs. 1991. *Disarmament Bulletin* (Fall).

Eguizábal, Cristina, ed. 1988. *América Latina y la crisis centroamericana: en busca de una solución regional.* Buenos Aires: Grupo de Estudios Latinoamericanos (GEL).

Elguea, Javier. 1989. "Seguridad internacional y desarrollo nacional: la búsqueda de un concepto." In *En busca de la seguridad perdida,* eds. Sergio Aguayo Quezada and Bruce M. Bagley. Mexico: Siglo Veintiuno.

English, John A. 1991. *The Canadian Army and the Normandy Campaign.* New York: Praeger.

Ferreira Vidrigal, Armando A. 1985. *A evolucâo do pensamento estratégico naval brasileiro.* Rio de Janeiro: Biblioteca do Exército.

Finlayson, Jock. 1989. "Canada as a Strategic Mineral Importer: The Problematical Minerals." In *The New Geopolitics of Minerals,* ed. David Haglund. Vancouver: University of British Columbia Press.

Garciá Sayá, Diego, ed. 1989. *Coca, cocaína y narcotráfico: Labernito en los Andes.* Limá: Comisión andina de juristas.

González, Margarita. 1985. *Bolívar y la independencia de Cuba.* Bogotá: El Ancora.

Granatstein, J. L. 1977. *Ties that Bind: Canadian-American Relations in Wartime from the Great War to the Cold War.* Toronto: Stevens Hakkert.

Granatstein, J.L. 1991. *War and Peacekeeping: From South Africa to the Gulf.* Toronto: Key Porter.

Hertoghe, Alain, and Alain Lebrousse. 1989. *Le sentier lumineux du Pérou.* Pans: Découverte.

Hertling, Mark. 1990. "Narcoterrorism, the New Unconventional War." *Military Review* (March).

Humphreys, R. A. 1981. *Latin America and the Second World War 1939-1943.* London: Institute of Latin American Studies.

Jenkins, Gareth. 1991. "Western Europe and Cuba's Development in the 1980s and Beyond." In *Cuban Foreign Policy Confronts a New International Order,* eds. H.M. Grisman and John M. Kirk. Boulder, Colo.: Lynne Rienner.

Jockel, Joseph. 1987. *No Boundaries Upstairs.* Vancouver: University of British Columbia Press.

Klepak, H.P. 1986. "A Military Retreat from Politics in Latin America." *Armed Forces* (November).

Klepak, H.P. 1990. *Canada and Latin America: Strategic Issues for the 1990s.* Ottawa: Operational Research and Analysis Establishment (ORAE).

Klepak, H.P. 1990a. *Security Considerations and Verification of a Central American Arms Control Regime.* Ottawa: Department of External Affairs.

Klepak, H.P. 1991. "Hard Times Ahead for Havana." *Jane's Defense Weekly.* October 12.

Klepak, H.P. 1992. "Le tango de la dénucléarisation: le duo Argentine et Brésil." In *La Prolifération nucléaire dans les années 1990,* eds. Albert Legault and Michel Fortmann. Québec: Centre québécois de relations internationales.

Klepak, H.P. 1992a. "Remaining Obstacles to Peace in Central America." *Notes Stratégiques 2,* St. Jean: The Queen's Printer.

Knippers-Black, Jan. 1982. *Sentinels of Europe.* New York: Greenwood.

Lane, Charles. 1992. "The Newest War." *Newsweek.* January 6.

Lefeber, Walter. 1983. *Inevitable Revolutions.* New York: Norton.

López, Ernesto. 1987. *Seguridad nacional y sedición militar.* Buenos Aires: Legasa.

Lowenthal, Abraham. 1987. *Partners in Conflict.* Baltimore: Johns Hopkins.

Mabry, Donald J. 1989. "The Role of the U.S. Military in the War on Drugs." In *The Latin American Narcotics Trade and U.S. National Security,* ed. Donald J. Mabry. New York: Greenwood.

MacKenzie, David. 1991. "The World's Greatest Joiner, Canada and the Organization of American States." *British Journal of Canadian Studies* VI:1.

Martins, Dean. 1990. *Non-proliferation Policy and Nuclear Threshold States: The Case of Argentina and Brazil.* Kingston: Queens University (unpublished thesis).

Mercado Jarrin, Edgardo. 1987. "Perspectivas de los acuerdos de limitación y desarme en América Latina y el Caribe." In *Paz, desarme y desarrollo en América Latina,* ed. Augusto Varas. Buenos Aires: GEL.

Mercado Jarrin, Edgardo. 1989. *Un sistema de seguridad y defensa sudamericano.* Lima: Centro Peruano de Estudios Internacionales (CEPEI).

Moneta, Carlos. 1990. "Pensamiento y acción latinoamericana ante las fuerzas armadas. Percepciones, conductas tradicionales y nuevas alternaciones." In *Civiles y militares: fuerzas armadas y transición democrática,* ed. Carlos Moneta. Caracas: Nueva Sociedad.

Moral, Roberto Noel. 1989. *Ayacucho: Testimonio de un soldado.* Lima: Publinor.

Morton, Desmond. 1985. *The Military History of Canada.* Edmonton: Hurtig.

North, Liisa. 1990. *Between War and Peace in Central America: Choices for Canada*. Toronto: Between the Lines.

Nunn, Frederick. 1985. *Yesterday's Soldiers*. Lincoln: University of Nebraska Press.

Ogelsby, J.C.M. 1976. *Gringos from the Far North*. Toronto: Macmillan.

"ONUCA OBSERVER." 1991. Tegucigalpa: Lithopress.

Palma, Hugo. 1986. *América Latina: Limitación de armamento y desarme en la región*. Lima: CEPEI.

Portales, Carlos. 1987. "Seguridad regional en Sudamérica. Escenarios prospectivos." In *Paz, desarme y desarrollo en América Latina,* ed. Augusto Varas. Buenos Aires: GEL.

Queille, Pierre. 1969. *L'Amérique Latine, la Doctrine Monroe et la panaméricanisme*. Paris: Payot.

Reynolds, Clark, and Stephen Wager. 1990. "Integración económica de México y Estados Unidos: Implicaciones para la seguridad de ambos países." In *En busca de la seguridad perdida,* eds. Sergio Aguayo Quezada and Bruce M. Bagley. Mexico: Siglo Veintiuno.

Rizzo de Oliveira, E., et al. 1987. *As forças armadas no Brazil*. Rio de Janeiro: Espaço e tempo.

Russell, Roberto. 1990. "Argentina: ¿una nueva política exterior?" In *El Desafío de los '90,* ed. Heraldo Muñoz. Caracas: Nueva Sociedad.

Schoultz, Lars. 1987. *National Security and United States Policy Toward Latin America*. Princeton: Princeton University Press.

Segue, Magdalena, and Héctor E. Bocco. 1990. "Brasil: el fin de temporada." In *El Desafío de los '90,* ed. Heraldo Muñoz. Caracas: Nueva Sociedad.

Toro, Maria Celia. 1989. "Mexico y Estados Unidos: el narcotráfico como amenaza a la seguridad nacional." In *En busca de la seguridad perdida,* eds. Sergio Aguayo Quezada and Bruce M. Bagley. Mexico: Siglo Veintiuno.

Varas, Augusto. 1987. "De la competencia a la cooperación militar en América Latina." In *Paz, desarme y desarrollo en América Latina,* ed. Augusto Varas. Buenos Aires: GEL.

Varas, Augusto. 1988. *"Autonomización castrense y democracia en América Latina. In *La autonomía militar en América Latina,* ed. Augusto Varas. Caracas: Nueva Sociedad.

Veneroni, Horacio, 1973. *Estados Unidos y las fuerzas amadas en América Latina*. Buenos Aires: Periferia.

Werneck Sodré, Nelson. 1979. *A historia militar do Brasil*. Rio de Janeiro: Civilzação brasileira.

CONCLUSION: THE FUTURE CHALLENGE

Edgar J. Dosman and Jerry Haar

The dramatic change in Canadian foreign policy toward Latin America since 1990 reflects a long-term shift in orientation and priorities. A major re-ordering of Canadian external relations is underway, in which the Western Hemisphere has become a region of new opportunities, challenges, and responsibilities.

Traditionally, Canada has been "northern" in its foreign policy orientation. The post-World War II focus was overwhelmingly centered on the United States, Europe, and later the Pacific; NATO, NORAD, OECD, the United Nations, and the GATT were the principal "northern clubs" in which Canadian security, economic, and political interests were well-served. In contrast, Latin America — notwithstanding a century-long commercial and missionary relationship — remained on the fringe of Canadian foreign relations. Ottawa was relieved to remain outside the tension-ridden atmosphere of U.S.-Latin American relations, which it neither understood nor liked.

In short, Canada's self-image was in no sense of the word "inter-American." Only with the Commonwealth Caribbean and Haiti had "special relationships" emerged; and these were marginal exceptions in the overall policy framework. For their part, the major Latin American countries viewed Canada as an attractive, friendly northern outpost of the United States lacking a market worth pursuing, with Ottawa a convenient diplomatic destination for politicos too hot to handle at home. Thus, from 1945 through the "lost decade" of the 1980s, an unfortunate pattern developed in Canadian-Latin American relations: blips of reciprocal interest heralding "new partnerships" and "third options" would be followed by mutual neglect, most recently following the arrival of the debt crisis after 1982. Canadian-Latin American relations seemed fated to remain shallow, lacking conviction and intensity — including those with Mexico (such an obvious partner given the U.S. connection), where trade and investment relations during the 1980s languished.

Today, three years later, the landscape has completely changed. In commercial affairs, Canada's Embassy in Mexico City is one of the busiest posts abroad, with forty-five hundred business inquiries in 1992. Latin American hot-line business calls in Canada now equal those from the United States. Canada is the world's largest investor in Chile. NAFTA, whether the present agreement is ratified or not, has already produced a permanent change in Canadian-Mexican relations. Politically, Canada's entrance into the OAS in 1990 reflects its acceptance of membership in the inter-American system, demonstrated most visibly by a quantum jump in Canada's security involvement in the Americas.

If there is no longer a question of whether Canada is, at last, an "inter-American" participant, the quality and direction of that involvement is only now being defined. As Ottawa and the Canadian population struggle to elaborate a coherent inter-American policy to help shape the emerging economic and political architecture of the Western Hemisphere, the internal and external challenges facing Canada in the pre-occupying uncertainty of the post-Cold War world both assist and limit its role in region-building in the Americas.

The Economic Dimension

The NAFTA process, much more than OAS membership, provided the essential catalyst for changing the nature of Canadian-Latin American relations. It opened corporate and government eyes to new trade liberalization and macroeconomic policies in Mexico and the region as well as their significance for future economic relations between Canada and Latin America. In personal terms, NAFTA negotiations forged close relationships between Mexican and Canadian corporate leaders and officials; the inevitable boom industry for economists and consultants rapidly followed.

If traditionally Canada's business presence in Mexico and Latin America had been dominated by a small number of transnational firms in banking, mining, and consulting engineering with few linkages to Canadian corporations — particularly small and medium-sized enterprises (SMEs) — NAFTA established the knowledge infrastructure for a more broadly based interest in Mexico. Corporate Canada awoke to the reality of a large Spanish-speaking market with US$334 billion GDP that was quite open to Canadian participation and technology. The response of Canadian SMEs has been exceptional, from British Columbia to the Atlantic. Five hundred companies were mobilized for trade shows in Mexico; a specialized event such as ANTAD 1993 in

Guadalajara dealing with food-processing drew sixty-eight Canadian firms. Interest in South America, particularly Chile but increasingly also Argentina, Venezuela, and Colombia is also intense. No longer are merely the larger international companies, such as Northern Telecom, SPAR, Bombardier, Simons International, SNC-Lavalin, Placer Dome, and the chartered banks, identified with Canada's corporate presence in Latin America.

The new Canadian corporate interest in Mexico and Latin America, however, is more profound than NAFTA negotiations, which served as catalyst rather than cause. Instead, the new activism is the result of external and internal factors gathering force in the 1980s. More particularly, the formation of regional trade groupings in Europe and Asia, on the one hand, and the opening of the Canadian economy in CUSFTA, on the other, finally forced Canadian business to look beyond local markets for survival in the new global economy. In this new optic, Mexico and Latin America have an obvious and special place given their market size, growth prospects, and degree of international openness.

A coherent, explicit Canadian economic policy for the hemisphere in cooperation with the private sector would facilitate a stronger, positive role in the region and realize current opportunities. Many LAC countries have undergone sweeping economic changes: the debt crisis is now being managed effectively in the region; trade and investment liberalization, financial market reform, labor market reform, and the privatization of the public sector continue. With the crisis now under control, there is greater scope for Canadian trade and investment opportunities as well as the opportunity to play a role in bolstering these reforms.

Needless to say, international competitors are similarly aware of these new market opportunities. In this exceptionally competitive environment, Canadian firms, private sector associations, and government agencies are now struggling to make up for missed opportunities with new approaches in trade promotion and joint ventures. Several initiatives, such as the establishment of the private-sector managed Canadian Business Centre in Mexico City, are very promising indeed. There are also important business successes in telecommunications, informatics, machinery, and engineering. Two-way trade with Mexico has increased from US$2.4 to US$3.5 billion from 1990 to 1992. Even in the case of Brazil, despite the political confusion of the last years,

Canadian exports have grown by over 30 percent since 1990 to US$1.3 billion. Provincial governments — most notably Quebec, which has increased the size of its Mexican Office to twenty-six officials and designed a special action-plan to enhance access to the Mexican market — are helping companies forge permanent links in Latin America. In fact, the small province of Saskatchewan actually outsold Quebec and Alberta in the Mexican market in 1992, and companies in the Atlantic region are surprisingly competitive in Latin America and the Caribbean. By the end of the 1990s, bilateral trade with Mexico is estimated to be US$5 billion.

Notwithstanding the awakening and advances of the last three years, the challenge confronting the expansion of Canadian economic relations with Latin American partners is enormous. First, Canadian trade and investment starts from a small base. Now over three-quarters of Canadian trade is with the United States; Latin America and the Caribbean account for less than 5 percent, and a third of this is with Mexico where the trade deficit is US$2 billion in Mexico's favor. Second, while Canadian private foreign investment in Latin America and the Caribbean has a long tradition and is quite substantial ($8 billion in 1989, which exceeded investment in Europe outside the United Kingdom), an institutionalized myopia regarding opportunities in Latin America continued through the "lost decade" of the 1980s. With less than fifty Canadian firms responsible for more than two-thirds of the business activity in the region, the overall Canadian corporate presence has a narrow base. Of course, this can change rapidly, as the dramatic rise in Chilean investment demonstrates.

However, in general, there is a substantial knowledge gap through-out Canada regarding Latin America, particularly in business associations, technology institutes, and MBA programs. While "partnering" programs in these areas have been initiated, they are only a first step in the right direction. To compete effectively against U.S., European, or Asia-Pacific rivals, Canada must develop comparable habits of business/government/ research cooperation behind priority investment strategies and an equally deep framework of long-term cooperation in the knowledge and cultural sectors. Traditional trade promotion methods from the days of selling wheat and potash are definitively passé.

NAFTA is also important on a broader, regional level. Canada should use the agreement, and its anticipated increase in linkages with Mexico, as a vehicle to access the rest of the hemisphere, beginning with Chile. The Mexican government views the agreement as a first step in a regional strategy. So should Canada. There has already been much speculation on the prospects for NAFTA expansion, but whether the U.S. Congress approves it or not, Canada should move forward to enhance its role in the Americas. By pursuing a strong economic presence and gaining experience in Mexico, Canadian business can more effectively seek opportunities in other parts of the region.

The basic ingredients for successfully accessing inter-American markets have now been established. On the policy side, the region has been recognized as a priority, and it is also acknowledged that Canada's economic role in the Americas will not grow by itself. In particular, technology-based industries have the opportunity to broaden and expand their presence in the LAC markets, and firms not yet in the market can take advantage of current opportunities and potential benefits of regional trade integration and multilateralism. However, the problem confronting both the public and private sectors is implementation, particularly the availability of resources for enhanced trade and invest- ment promotion in the Americas. Canada is only now emerging from its deepest recession since the 1930s. As the country moves into the post- Mulroney era, it is hoped that government priorities continue to reflect the new salience of Latin America. In any case, a concerted effort is required to take full advantage of these opportunities, regardless of the Clinton administration's approach to NAFTA. Whatever happens in U.S. domestic politics, Canada's long-term interest in the Americas is to pursue trade liberalization with its new hemisphere partners.

The Political Dimension

If the reorganization of the international economy is increasingly forcing Canada to address markets in the Americas, the apparent rise of regional economic blocs confronts Canada with the need to look at the Americas as an emerging political community. This is also a novel foreign policy challenge, since Canada has traditionally relied on bilateral relationships, particularly with the stronger republics such as Mexico and Brazil. While these bilateral ties enjoyed periods of advance during years of expansion and growth — most notably, during the 1976-82 period when Pierre Elliot Trudeau was Prime Minister — they did not constitute a regional vision. Their fragility was demon- strated during the 1980s when Central America, a subregion of minimal national interest, became the centerpiece of Canadian policy toward Latin America as a whole.

The "new look" in Canadian-Latin American relations since 1990 is most evident with respect to NAFTA negotiations. This process, which has pushed Central America deep into the background, is important on two levels. First, emerging market forces and trilateralism with the United States in trade and investment decision-making suggest a long-term shift in patterns of governance within North America. As Blank and Waverman have pointed out in this volume, a changing architecture would affect the smaller partners much more than the dominant United States. In Canada, for example, West Coast or Québec integration with proximate U.S. states could exacerbate regional tensions at the expense of federal authority.

Second, and as a counterbalancing factor, the NAFTA process opens a substantively new bilateral relationship between Canada and Mexico. Through NAFTA negotiations, both governments have come to realize their mutual interests in strengthening bilateral relations to balance the new trilateralism. Obviously the U.S. connection will remain paramount for both Canada and Mexico, and there are important areas where interests diverge. But Canada and Mexico now need each other, and their mutual interests will grow rather than diminish. By the beginning of the next decade, Mexico will be of greater importance for Canadian foreign policy than Britain or France.

The end of the Cold War and the collapse of the Soviet Union have also accelerated the pace of Canada's political entrance in the Americas. One of the central features of Canada's foreign and defense policies has been the search for a counterweight to the friendly but rather overwhelming U.S. presence next door. NORAD and the Western Alliance against the Soviet threat were an invaluable tool in this balancing act. The elimination of the long-standing East-West tensions removes one entire plank of Canada's traditional Atlantic connection with Western Europe. With no enemies, the essential geographic reality — Canada as an inter-American country — is unchallengeable.

In other words, Canada has no option but to adjust to a new world order in which traditional groupings and alliances, such as NATO, have decreased considerably in importance. Its diplomatic response, therefore, has been predictable: to strengthen regional institutions — particularly, the OAS — and to become an active partner in inter-American security. Just as the Canadian objective in NAFTA is to strengthen rule-making to achieve the predictability in trade-regimes required by middle-powers for their survival and success, so Canada (in its modest way) views stable and strong governance in the Americas as essential for a healthy inter-American system of which it is now a part. Thus, Canadian leadership in elections monitoring, peacekeeping, and the peaceful resolution of disputes will likely remain an important element in its future policy in the region — both in and beyond Central America and the Caribbean. Its support for emerging democracies will also continue to help prevent the reemergence of military dictatorships and their associated lack of respect for human rights.

Canada's full membership in the OAS also fits well with the Canadian preference for acting through multilateral institutions as it offers many opportunities for increased Canadian involvement in issues, such as human rights and the promotion of and support for democracy. Moreover, there are many new challenges in the region that can be met effectively through institutions such as the OAS and its agencies. These include non-traditional regional security issues, such as illegal drug trafficking and environmental degradation — important areas which cannot be ignored and where Canada can make a significant contribution.

Canada's activist role in the OAS, its two large peace-keeping operations in Central America, and its militant posture in the ongoing Haitian debacle mark a stunning *volte-face* in Canadian foreign policy. The dimensions of this political departure, as both Stephen Randall and Hal Klepak have underlined, remain incalculable. Canada's middle-power instinct and imperative confront the reality of a policy and institutional vacuum in which important tensions and uncertainties remain in U.S.-Latin American relations despite their exceptional progress in recent years, including drug and migration issues, Cuba, human rights and democracy, and Central America. Canada is not only a new player in the Americas, it is also small relative to the United States. Yet, as with trade relations, it cannot avoid — in its own interests — responsibility for community-building.

Constituency: The Social and Cultural Dimension

The domestic constituency supporting the new thrust of Canadian foreign policy in Latin America and the Caribbean is similarly in transition. Unlike the United States, the Canadian government has enjoyed a high degree of autonomy from immigrant communities in the region, which remain small and without significant political influence over regional policy: there is nothing comparable in Ottawa to the pressure of the Cuban-American "Miami Lobby" in Washington. As a worldwide haven for refugees, Canada became a destination of choice for Chileans and Argentineans fleeing right-wing dictatorships, but there is now a broad political spectrum represented within the growing Latin American and Caribbean communities throughout the country. The key element is that they are growing, as migration from the region continues, and a stronger presence in all sectors is evident. The Haitian community in Montreal, or the West Indian in Toronto, may be the most visible symptoms of political clout. But compared with the entrenched and powerful European-Canadian associations pressing for initiatives and aid to the former Eastern Bloc countries, Latin American immigrants are heavily out-muscled.

The strongest non-governmental advocates for activism in Latin America, however, have been Canadian NGOs rather than immigrant associations. Since the 1970s, there has been an explosion of NGO linkages with counterparts in the region, particularly in Central America. Support groups with strong media and political connections — linked to the churches, community groups, and trade unions — combined in the 1980s to mount a formidable campaign for Canadian involvement in the promotion of human rights and democracy, development assistance, and the peace process. Idealistic and energetic, NGOs achieved an extraordinary visibility for Central American issues. In contrast, the business community seemed dormant, focusing its attention on the Canada-U.S. free trade debate, Europe, and Asia-Pacific — the last being the new magnet of attention in international trade. The effect of this lack of balance, compounded by exceptionally weak media capacity, was a distorted public image of Latin America as a nest of war and problems rather than as a potential economic partner with significant technological capacity.

Since 1990 the business constituency for Mexico and Latin America has changed dramatically as the Canadian private sector has awakened to its economic potential. This is an historic break with the past and a necessary ingredient for long-term community-building in the Americas. Overstatement should be avoided: so far only Mexico and Chile have been permanently incorporated into Canadian corporate strategic thinking, and political or economic setbacks — not improbable in the present Latin American environment — could dampen business enthusiasm. However, a threshold has been crossed; the private sector constituency is here to stay, and that is good news for Canada's emerging Latin American policy.

Nevertheless, major problems within Canada and the domestic constituency may limit the national capacity for its optimal insertion within the Americas. First, in a peculiar Canadian irony, the NAFTA debate pits the NGOs and private sector — the two strongest groups within the Canadian constituency — squarely against one another in a bitter debate. The NGOs denounce it as a sell-out, while the private sector views it as essential for survival. The absence of dialogue and the widespread public belief that CUSFTA caused massive job losses have damaged the understanding of NAFTA's broader significance. Trapped by an unrelenting hostility toward NAFTA, yet incorporating so much of the idealistic streak in Canadian foreign policy, the NGO community finds itself without the new vision for the Americas that the business community has discovered through necessity. The loss for Canada is a mobilization of both camps for both new initiatives toward Latin America and the Caribbean.

Second, regional and constitutional bickering have plagued Canada since 1990, fueling alienation in the West, nationalism in Quebec, and a general public uneasiness among Canadians everywhere. Coinciding with a brutal recession that has changed the landscape of industrial Canada (the outcome of which remains uncertain), regional discontent has affected Ottawa's capacity to orchestrate a coherent approach in inter-American affairs. Regarding NAFTA, Quebec and Alberta loudly applaud; Ontario and British Columbia dissent. Their inability to agree on inter-provincial trade hampers Canadian competitiveness and retraining programs. There are also positive signs, however, and much of the malaise will disappear with the end of the recession. Canadians accept that Quebec is a special political community in the Americas that desires a distinct relationship with Haiti and certain Latin American countries. The cultural ties between "Latin" Quebec and Hispanic America may be more perception than reality, but Quebec's four offices in Latin America and its numerous inter-governmental agreements and programs embody a specifically Québecois hemispheric projection. The positive side is Quebec activism in Latin America; the negative aspect relates to the continuing constitutional uncertainty in Canada.

Third, the growing assertiveness of Canada's aboriginal peoples is a reminder of a fundamental inter-American commonality — the European conquest and its bleak aftermath everywhere in the Americas where native populations survived. Canadian aboriginal peoples, however, don't need the reminder. Their linkages across boundaries, to the circumpolar north and south into the Americas, are already strong and will intensify in the 1990s and beyond. Aboriginal solidarity agreements, most recently between the Cree of Northern Quebec and Guatemalan Mayans, should not be underestimated in their long-term significance. The positive aspects of this hemispheric revival are potentially enormous. But the short-term effects of a public policy area of such urgency and cost may be a turning inward of federal and provincial governments — dealing with problems at home rather than foreign affairs.

The same effect may result from a fourth factor: the social tensions and violence arising from unemployment, poverty, ethnic unrest, and urban problems in general. Canada's generous refugee and immigration policy, along with educational systems and the extensive social safety net, were geared to assumptions of economic growth and the old economy where unskilled labor was abundant. Currently, as with other industrial countries, an overhaul of government and the public sector is taking place in adjustment to the transformation of business and industry. Some Canadians worry that the new architecture of the Americas may "harmonize away" their unique public institutions that define Canada's way of life in the Americas, leaving them with the unsuccessful and violence-prone cities that litter the Western Hemisphere. Still others see the present opening to the Americas as an opportunity to enrich the Canadian heritage in a reorganized New World.

Conclusion

What do inter-American relations mean for Canada in the 1990s? To what extent can Canada play a useful role with its Latin and Caribbean partners? To what extent does this affect its U.S. relationship? To what extent does Latin American interest in Canada complement Canadian interests? Certainly, Canada can no longer avoid bold initiatives and a strategic approach to realize the potential benefits of Canadian-Latin American relations in the 1990s.

By building on traditional Canadian roles in the region through multilateral institutions, as well as addressing the emerging social and security challenges in the region, there is much scope for a growing Canadian presence in the Americas. In fact, one could argue that Canadian activity in these areas of expertise in the future will serve as an educational beacon for both the United States and the nations of Latin America and the Caribbean. Conversely, these nations, including the United States, can play an important educational and cultural awareness role for Canadian troops and organizations that may not be familiar with issues particular to the Latin American and Caribbean context.

Canada's potential contribution to the political evolution of the Americas lies in projecting those values which permitted it to prosper with two political communities — French and English — and increasingly vocal aboriginal peoples alongside a superpower — namely, democracy, tolerance, a European-style social awareness, and a new-world adaptability. Even though internal problems have placed the survival of these values in question, it is important to recognize the unique position that Canada holds in the hemisphere. Canada has felt the profound economic influence of the United States as much as any other country in the region, but it has profited from the relationship. Nevertheless, Canadians recognize the need to seek alternatives in many economic and cultural areas. It is precisely here where Canada can help share this alternative vision with the countries and peoples of Latin America and the Caribbean to the mutual benefit of all.

ABOUT THE EDITORS

JERRY HAAR is senior research associate and director of the Canada Program and the Inter-American Business and Labor Program at the University of Miami's North-South Center. Dr. Haar was director of Washington programs for the Council of the Americas, a New York-based business association of over two hundred U.S. corporations with private investment in Latin America, and has also held several senior staff positions with the federal government in policy planning, management evaluation, and organizational development. After graduating from the School of International Service at The American University, Dr. Haar was a Fulbright scholar at the Getúlio Vargas Foundation School of Public Administration in Rio de Janeiro, Brazil. He also holds graduate degrees from Johns Hopkins, Columbia, and Harvard universities and has authored or co-authored a number of books and scholarly articles.

EDGAR J. DOSMAN, director of the Canada-Latin America Forum, Ottawa, Canada, was raised and educated in the province of Saskatchewan. Following graduate studies at University College, Oxford, Harvard University, and the University of Munich, Germany, he became professor of international relations at York University, Toronto, and chair of its department of political science. Professor Dosman is a fellow of the Centre for Research on Latin America and the Caribbean and has published widely in the field of inter-American relations and Latin American affairs. He has served as consultant to a wide variety of Canadian, inter-American, and international agencies and organizations.

ABOUT THE PUBLISHER

THE NORTH-SOUTH CENTER promotes better relations among the United States, Canada, and the nations of Latin America and the Caribbean. The Center provides a disciplined, intellectual focus for improved relations, commerce, and understanding in the hemisphere, wherein major political, social, and economic issues are seen in a global perspective. The Center conducts programs of education, training, cooperative study, public outreach, and research and engages in an active program of publication and dissemination of information on the Americas. The North-South Center fosters linkages among academic and research institutions throughout the Americas and acts as an agent of change in the region.

Ambler H. Moss, Jr
Director, North-South Center

Richard Downes
Communications Director

Kathleen A. Hamman
Editorial Director

Mary M. Mapes
Publications Director

Jayne M. Weisblatt
Editor

Gloria Gómez-Canteñs
Production Assistant

PRODUCTION NOTES

This book was printed on 60 lb. Phoenix Opaque Natural, 420 PPI, opacity 95, smooth finish text stock with a 10 point CIS cover stock.

The text of this volume was set in Garamond, with Avant Garde headlines and subheads, at the North-South Center's Publications Department, using Aldus Pagemaker 4.2, on a Macintosh LC II computer. It was formatted by Gloria Gómez-Canteñs.

The cover was created by Mary M. Mapes using Aldus Freehand 3.1 for the illustration and QuarkXPress 3.11 for the composition and color separation.

The book was edited by Jayne M. Weisblatt.

This publication was printed by Edwards Brothers, Inc. of Lillington, North Carolina.